Erin Hentzel

# Doll Studio BOUTIQUE

## SEW A WARDROBE

46 Garments & Accessories for 14″ Dolls

FunStitch
STUDIO
an imprint of C&T Publishing

PUBLISHER: Amy Barrett-Daffin

CREATIVE DIRECTOR: Gailen Runge

ACQUISITIONS EDITOR: Roxane Cerda

MANAGING EDITOR: Liz Aneloski

EDITOR: Beth Baumgartel

TECHNICAL EDITOR: Helen Frost

COVER/BOOK DESIGNER: April Mostek

PRODUCTION COORDINATOR: Tim Manibusan

PRODUCTION EDITOR: Jennifer Warren

ILLUSTRATOR: Mary E. Flynn

PHOTO ASSISTANT: Gabriel Martinez

COVER PHOTOGRAPHY by Sydney Paulsen

INSTRUCTIONAL PHOTOGRAPHY by Estefany Gonzalez and Lauren Herberg of C&T Publishing, Inc.; LIFESTYLE PHOTOGRAPHY by Sydney Paulsen and SUBJECTS PHOTOGRAPHY by Page + Pixel, unless otherwise noted

Published by FunStitch Studio, an imprint of C&T Publishing, Inc., P.O. Box 1456, Lafayette, CA 94549

Library of Congress Cataloging-in-Publication Data

Names: Hentzel, Erin, 1966- author.

Title: Doll studio boutique : sew a wardrobe; 46 garments & accessories for 14" dolls / Erin Hentzel.

Description: Lafayette : FunStitch Studio, [2021]

Identifiers: LCCN 2021015813 | ISBN 9781644030882 (trade paperback) | ISBN 9781644030899 (ebook)

Subjects: LCSH: Doll clothes--Patterns. | Miniature craft. | Sewing.

Classification: LCC TT175.7 .H468 2021 | DDC 745.592/21--dc23

LC record available at https://lccn.loc.gov/2021015813

Printed in China

10 9 8 7 6 5 4 3 2 1

## Dedication

*For my older sister, Maureen, who would hand sew and embroider for hours, and would always let me sit and watch.*

## Acknowledgments

A special thanks to my family: I love you and am grateful for each of you.

To Amy, Liz, Roxane, Beth, Gailen, Lauren, Helen, Jennifer, Mary, Gabriel, April, and Tim for their expertise and talent that helped make my book amazing.

To Art Gallery Fabrics, Benartex, Clothworks, Dear Stella, and Timeless Treasures, who generously provided me with their beautiful fabrics with which to create many projects for my book.

Special thanks to Cherry Guidry for making the graphics to match her fabric collection, Planted with Love, that I used with TAP to create special outfits for my dolls to wear in this book, and to Sydney Paulsen, it was such a joy to meet you and work with you; your photos are extraordinary.

# Contents

## PROJECTS

### SKIRTS

*Simple Skirts*

*Twirl Skirts*

### TOPS

*Simple Tops*

*Swing Tank Tops*

*Raglan Tops*

## BOTTOMS

*Simple Shorts and Pants*

50

## DRESSES

*Sundresses*

57

*Classic Sleeveless Dress*

67

*Vintage Party Dress*

75

## KNITWEAR

*Fitted T-Shirt and Fit and Flare Dress*

83

## SLEEPWEAR

*PJ Sets and Nightgown*

87

*Slippers*

95

## ACCESSORIES

*Headbands*

98

*Tote Bags*

102

*Bucket Hat*

107

# Introduction

A complete wardrobe of doll clothes and accessories are modeled on three different brands of dolls throughout this book. The garments are designed specifically for 14½″ dolls; however, most designs also fit 14″–15″ (similarly shaped) dolls nicely.

This book was written with the beginner in mind, so the projects focus on general sewing techniques for seven basic designs—skirts, tops, bottoms, knitwear, dresses, sleepwear, and accessories—as well as numerous variations. More experienced seamstresses will love the quick-to-sew designs as well as the advanced beginner and beyond beginner projects. No matter your sewing level, you will have plenty of patterns with which to create a complete wardrobe for your own, or for someone else's, 14½″ doll.

## How to Use This Book

General Sewing (page 14) and Sewing Techniques (page 16) are your go-to reference chapters when you need more detailed instructions. These chapters include photo tutorials of many techniques that are used throughout this book. They explain everything you'll need to get started and keep going!

Many of the projects use the same techniques. Instead of repeating the same instructions every time a technique is required to make a project, there is a page reference to the technique within the project instructions.

## Sewing Levels

Every project features an icon that indicates the recommended sewing level for each project. The icons will help you decide which projects to begin with if you are new to sewing. Start with a beginner project and build your skills with more advanced projects! In this way you will gain confidence, challenge yourself, and develop your sewing skills in a natural progression.

⦿ **BEGINNER:** You are beginning to learn how to sew on a machine.

⦿◖ **CONFIDENT BEGINNER:** You are comfortable with the machine, have sewn several simple projects, and are ready to do more than straight seams.

⦿⦿ **INTERMEDIATE BEGINNER:** You've got basic skills and are ready to learn some different techniques, like gathering.

⦿⦿⦿ **ADVANCED BEGINNER:** You have more than the basic skills and are ready to learn more, like sewing tiny sleeves.

⦿⦿⦿⦿ **BEYOND BEGINNER:** You can pretty much sew any of the projects, and, though a couple steps may be challenging, you're ready to learn.

# Tools and Supplies

The proper tools sometimes make all the difference in your sewing success, and sometimes they even make a specific technique easier.

## SEWING KIT

A basic sewing kit is all you need for most of the projects. It's a good idea to have a basket or container to store the tools and supplies you need for sewing.

**A** **DRESSMAKER'S SHEARS:** A bent-handle design helps keep the fabric from lifting off the table while cutting.

- **Note** Owning a variety of fabric scissors and shears is important because they all have different uses. Use them to cut only fabric and you will be grateful.

**B** **4″ SCISSORS:** Shorter-length scissors with sharp blades work great for cutting angles, clipping edges, and trimming threads.

**C** **SEAM RIPPER:** Slide the hook at the base under a stitch to cut the thread. To remove a seam, cut every two or three stitches; then gently pull the fabric pieces apart.

**D PINKING SHEARS:** These make zigzag cuts to prevent edges from unraveling.

**E STRAIGHT PINS:** I prefer to use *silk pins*; these pins are .039″ (.5mm) in diameter and glide easily into the fabric. Use ballpoint pins for knit fabrics.

**F SAFETY PINS OR A BODKIN:** Use these to insert elastic or drawstrings into casings. You can also use a **LARGE BLUNT-TIP TAPESTRY NEEDLE** to insert elastic into smaller casings.

**G HAND SEWING NEEDLES:** Use these to sew small embellishments, such as bows and buttons.

**H SEWING MACHINE NEEDLES:** Match the needle to the fabric. Smaller-size needles are suitable for lightweight fabrics, while larger-size needles are best for heavier-weight fabrics.

## Sewing Machine Needles

▶ Use a universal needle for sewing most woven fabrics, such as quilting cotton.

▶ Use a stretch needle or ballpoint needle for sewing knit fabrics.

▶ Use a microtex needle for fine, tightly woven fabrics, such as Swiss Dot, lawn, and voile.

▶ Use a jeans needle for heavier-weight fabrics, such as denim, twill, and corduroy.

**I SEAM GAUGE:** Use this tool to measure consistently.

**J RULER:** Use this for marking cutting lines or fold lines.

**K FABRIC MARKERS:** Use these to transfer pattern markings. Your markings will disappear over time or with water.

**L CORNER-TURNING TOOL:** Use this tool for turning collars, bodices, and straps.

**M THREAD:** Use all-purpose polyester thread. Match the fabric color (or the background color on prints). *Note:* The samples have been sewn with contrasting thread for clarity.

**N TAPE MEASURE:** Use this for measuring things that are round, like a doll's waist.

## PRESSING

Your basic sewing tools should also include an iron and ironing surface.

### IRON

**SMALL IRONING BOARD (OR SLEEVE BOARD):** Doll clothes will fit over the end of a small board, like this handmade one by Etsy seller AdorablyDolly.

## SPECIALTY TOOLS

These extra tools are extremely helpful and make sewing these small projects much more manageable.

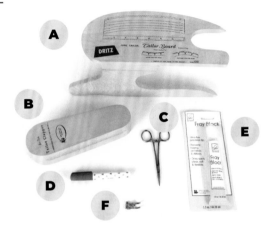

**A TAILOR BOARD:** This old-school tool has narrow pressing sections as well as rounded ones, which are great for curved seams.

**B CLAPPER:** Use this to make creases sharper without much effort.

**C HEMOSTAT:** These scissors-like tweezers can reach inside openings where your fingers cannot fit.

**D WONDER TAPE OR FABRIC GLUE STICK:** These help to hold tiny things, such as buttons and bows, in place instead of using pins.

**E FRAY BLOCK (by June Tailor):** My preferred brand of anti-fray sealant, this dries quickly and clear.

**F ¼″ (6MM) PRESSER FOOT:** This is perfect for sewing ¼″ seam allowances.

**TIP** If your ¼″ presser foot has a circular hole for the needle instead of an oblong-shaped opening, make sure you only use a straight stitch. Otherwise, the needle can hit the metal and break.

## ROTARY CUTTER, RULER, AND CUTTING MAT

Rotary cutting is an accurate way to quickly cut basic geometric shapes such as rectangles for straps or skirt pieces.

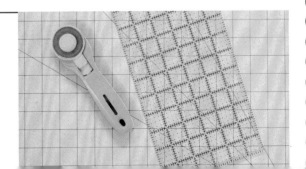

# Fabrics

Fabric affects the drape of a design as well as the silhouette/shape of the finished garment. Choose high-quality, soft-to-the-touch fabrics for best results.

## WOVEN FABRICS

Woven fabrics hold their shape because they don't stretch. They also tend to fray, so the raw edges will need to be finished. Woven fabrics suitable for making doll clothes include quilting cotton, poplin, chambray, twill, lawn, and linen.

## KNIT FABRICS

Knits are stretchy and don't fray, so the raw edges don't need to be finished. Good types of knits for sewing doll clothes include jersey, cotton LYCRA, and cotton spandex.

## FABRIC PRINT AND SCALE

*Fabric scale* refers to the size of the design motifs printed on the fabric. The smaller the doll, the smaller the scale of the print should be. Larger-scale prints look overwhelming in doll clothes. *Ditsy*, *micro*, and *mini prints* are search keywords to help you look online for appropriate fabrics for your doll projects.

Keep the embellishments, such as lace, trims, and buttons, smaller scale too. A rule of thumb is to imagine the ratio on a human garment: A 1″ button on a doll dress has the same impact as a 3″–4″ button on a dress designed for people.

## PRINT DIRECTION

Look carefully for any directional prints on the fabric—such as images of animals, trees, flower stems, and words—before cutting out the fabric pieces. If the fabric has directional motifs, pin and cut out all the pattern pieces facing the same direction. You don't want to accidentally end up with some—or all—of the motifs upside down when the garment is finished!

# Using a Pattern

Whenever you are sewing with a pattern, read all the directions first. Oftentimes a step becomes clearer when you read the sewing steps that immediately follow it. Before moving to the next step, reread the step you just did. It's easy to miss a little step or detail.

## WHAT'S ON THE PATTERN?

When you start to make a project, find all the necessary pattern pieces needed. They are listed in the project instructions under the Cutting list, and they all can be found on the pullout in the back of the book. The patterns can also be downloaded and printed at

*tinyurl.com/11442-patterns-download*.

Each pattern piece is labeled with the *project name*, *project part* (sleeve, bodice, and so on), and *pattern number*.

The pattern piece also indicates cutting instructions, information as to how it should be cut out, and how many pieces are needed for the project.

When the pattern's shape is a rectangle, the measurements are given instead of a pattern piece (see Cut Fabric Pieces Without Patterns, page 13).

## GRAIN

The *grainline* of woven fabric is basically the weave of the fabric, or the direction of the threads. For knits, the grain is the wales of the knitted fabric, lengthwise "columns" that run parallel to the selvage. It's important to place the patterns on the fabric so that the grainline markings are parallel to the fabric grainline—this ensures that the fabric behaves and drapes as the pattern intended.

The straight grainline of woven fabric is on the length; this is parallel to the finished selvage edges. These edges are often printed with the name of the fabric company and collection. The cross grain is on the width of the fabric, perpendicular to the selvage edges. True bias is at a 45° angle from the grainline and cross grain.

**TIP** Avoid the selvage when cutting the pattern pieces; you don't want it to be part of the finished project.

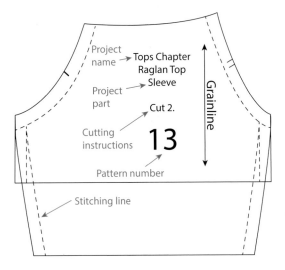

## PREPARE AND FOLD THE FABRIC

Sometimes you only need to cut a pattern one time, so you can cut it from a single layer of fabric.

More often, you need to cut a pattern two times. You will need to fold the fabric if the pattern indicates "Cut 1 on fold." or "Cut 2."

- Fold the fabric either right sides together or wrong sides together.

- If you are using scraps of fabric or two separate pieces of fabric, make sure to place them either right sides together or wrong sides together so you have left and right pieces.

- To fold the fabric in half, measure from the selvage edge to the fold in the fabric. Do this across the length of the fold, making sure the measurement remains the same.

## LAYOUT, PIN, AND CUT THE PATTERNS

*Arrange all the patterns on the fabric so you know how they fit. Place the grainline arrow parallel to the selvage edge. Pin the ends of the grainline arrow first and then pin the remainder of the pattern. Cut around the pattern on the cutting lines.*

Most patterns indicate "Cut 1." or "Cut 1 on fabric fold." or "Cut 2."

**CUT 1:** Cut the pattern from a single layer of fabric.

**CUT 1 ON FABRIC FOLD:** Fold the fabric so the fold is straight on the grainline. Pin the edge marked "Place on fold." on the fold first. Do not cut along the fold line.

**CUT 2:** Fold the fabric in half, with the selvage edges (or selvage to raw edge) even with the fold in the fabric.

**CUT ON THE BIAS:** Place the pattern piece on the diagonal of the fabric, keeping the grainline marking parallel to the selvage.

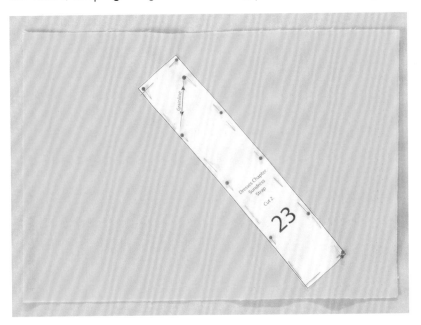

## CUT FABRIC PIECES WITHOUT PATTERNS

When a pattern piece is a rectangle, use the measurements provided in the project's Cutting list to cut out the fabric. Cut these pieces straight on the grain of fabric, with 2 opposing sides parallel to the selvage. Some people prefer to use a rotary cutter (page 9). You can also create a pattern piece using graph paper and a ruler, or use a fabric marker and ruler to draw the cutting lines directly onto the wrong side of the fabric.

## TRANSFER PATTERN MARKINGS

After cutting out the fabric pieces and before removing all the pins, use a fabric marker to transfer any important markings to the fabric, such as pleat lines, placement markings, or dots.

# General Sewing

## SEAM ALLOWANCE

The *seam allowance* is the distance from the stitching line to the raw edge. Most of the projects in this book use a ¼″ (6mm) seam allowance. You'll need to sew that seam allowance for the fabric pieces to fit together properly.

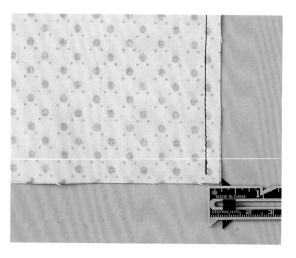

## STITCH LENGTH

Sew the seams on woven fabrics with a straight stitch. Set your machine length at 2.5 for most of the projects. Note that gathering stitches are longer.

Sew the seams on knit fabrics with a narrow zigzag stitch or stretch stitch if your machine has it.

### Sewing a Seam

Pin the fabric layers together to keep the pieces from shifting while you sew. Keep the raw edges even and place the pins perpendicular to the stitching line.

Keep edges even.

Slide the fabric under the presser foot and align the fabric edges with the seam allowance guideline. Always start and end a seam with backstitches, 2–3 stitches in reverse. This will prevent the stitches from coming out later.

## FINISHED SEAM ALLOWANCES

Finishing the raw edges of the fabric after sewing a seam prevents woven fabric from unraveling or fraying. Here are some of the ways in which to finish seam allowances.

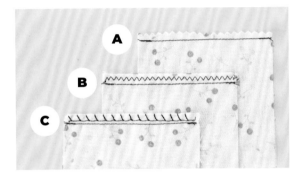

**A PINKED EDGE:** Use pinking shears to trim the raw edge of the fabric. Be careful not to cut the stitches of the seam.

**B ZIGZAG STITCH:** Sew a row of zigzag stitches within the seam allowance. It's okay to stitch over the raw edge, but don't stitch over the seam you've just sewn.

**C OVERCAST STITCH:** Many traditional sewing machines have an overcast stitch. It is more effective than using the zigzag stitch and less bulky than a serged edge.

## PRESS SEAM ALLOWANCES

Pressing seam allowances is an important step and can make sewing fabric pieces together easier. *Don't skip pressing ever.* When possible, press the seam allowances on both the right side and wrong side to get them nice and flat.

Seam allowances are either pressed open or to one side, depending on the project.

Seam allowances pressed open

Seam allowances pressed to one side

# Sewing Techniques

## HEMS

### Double-Fold Hem

The project instructions indicate specific folding measurements for each project that features a double-fold hem. If measurements are not provided, use a ½˝ (1cm) hem allowance as shown.

**TIP** Use a sewing gauge to measure as you fold and press for accurate and consistent hems.

**1.** Fold the fabric ¼˝ (6mm) to the wrong side and press.

**2.** Fold again ¼˝ (6mm) to the wrong side and press.

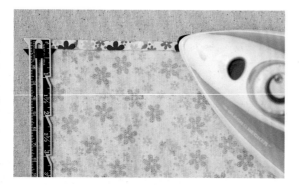

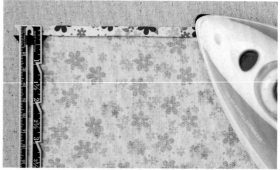

**3.** Sew across the folded fabric, close to the inside fold.

**TIP** Use a rolled-hem presser foot to sew hems that are even narrower. These will be less bulky and are perfect for garments with lots of gathers. For additional help, watch my video tutorial about using a rolled-hem presser foot; for the link, see Bonus Videos (page 112).

## Hem a Curved Edge / Narrow Hem

**1.** Fold and press the fabric to the wrong side of the fabric ¼˝ (6mm) or a little less. Work a small section at a time. As you press, work to maintain the curve of the raw edge.

**2.** Sew on the fold. Trim the raw edge to ⅛˝ (3mm).

**3.** Repeat Step 1 and sew on the folded edge. Press the finished hem.

## Hem with Trims

**1.** Pin and sew the trim to the piece, right sides together, with the trim upside down.

**2.** Finish the raw edges.

**3.** Fold and press the seam allowances toward the wrong side of the fabric. Topstitch.

**4.** When adding a trim that has finished edges, such as Cluny lace, rickrack, or picot trim, hem or finish the raw edge of the fabric before sewing the trim to it.

## SEW A CASING FOR ELASTIC

Casings for elastic are typically found at waistlines, sleeve hems, and pant-leg hems. They are sewn much like a double-fold hem.

**1.** Press the first fold ¼″ (6mm) to the wrong side.

**2.** Press the second fold; the width of the second fold should be at least ⅛″ (3mm) wider than the elastic to make inserting the elastic easier. Stitch close to the second fold, leaving a 2″ (5.1cm) opening for inserting the elastic if the casing is made in a loop. If the casing isn't in a loop, you can insert the elastic through either of the open ends.

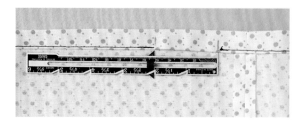

### *Insert the Elastic*

**1.** Attach a safety pin or bodkin to an end of the elastic. Insert the safety pin into the opening of the casing.

**2.** Push and scrunch the fabric with one hand as you push the safety pin farther into the casing with the other hand.

**3.** Hold onto the safety pin and smooth out the fabric behind it, releasing the gathers.

**4.** Feed and work the safety pin and elastic in this way until the safety pin comes out the other end. Keep an eye on the other end of the elastic. Pin it at the opening if it looks like it may be pulled into the casing while you work.

**TIP** Placing a safety pin on both ends of the elastic prevents you from having to start over if the end of the elastic disappears into the casing.

**5.** Once the safety pin comes out the other side of the opening, pull both ends of the elastic away from the casing to give yourself enough elastic to work with.

**6.** Overlap the ends and sew them together, making sure the elastic is not twisted.

**7.** Pull on the fabric to get the elastic inside the casing all the way. Sew the opening closed.

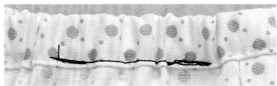

## MAKE STRAPS

### Straps Without Finished Ends

**1.** Fold the strap piece in half lengthwise and press.

**2.** Unfold the strap and fold the raw edges to the center crease. Press.

**3.** Fold lengthwise again, enclosing the raw edges, and press.

**4.** Edgestitch across the folded edge.

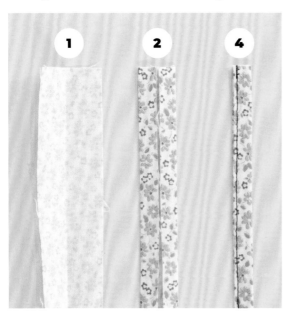

### Straps with Finished Ends

**1.** Follow Straps Without Finished Ends, Steps 1 and 2 (at left).

**2.** Fold in half lengthwise, with the raw edges on the outside.

**3.** Sew across one or both short end(s) as indicated in the project instructions. Trim the corners diagonally.

**4.** Turn right side out, use a corner-turning tool to gently poke out the corners, and press.

**5.** Edgestitch the long, open folded edge.

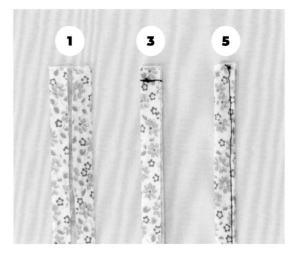

## GATHERING

The traditional method to gather fabric, shown here, is tried and true. For the best results and tighter gathers, sew the rows of gathering stitches on either side of the stitching line. For example, for a ¼˝ (6mm) seam allowance, sew one row ⅛˝ (3mm) from the raw edge and the second row ⅜˝ (1cm) from the raw edge.

**1.** Use a long stitch length to sew 2 rows of parallel straight stitches. Do not backstitch, and leave the thread tails at both ends long enough to hold.

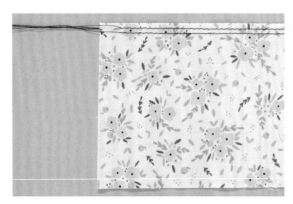

**2.** Pull on both bobbin threads at the same time to slide the fabric together and create the gathers.

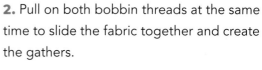

**3.** Once the fabric is the desired length, move the gathers loosely between finger and thumb to slide and distribute them more evenly. It helps to anchor the gathering threads by wrapping them around a pin placed at each end. The gathers can then be distributed all the way to these anchor points.

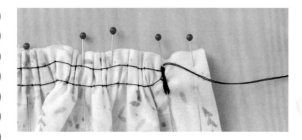

**4.** Pin and sew the gathered fabric to the other piece as directed. After the seam is sewn, gathering stitches can be removed.

Seam is red; gathering stitches are black.

**TIP** It's easier to sew back seams and closures when the fabric isn't gathered too closely to the center back edges. Start and stop the gathering about ½˝ (1.2cm) from the center back edges.

## SEWING CURVES

Curved seams require some special handling and finishing.

- Sew with a small stitch, setting the machine to a 1.5–2mm stitch length.

- Sew slowly, pivoting as needed with the needle down and the presser foot up.

- Cut triangle-shaped notches in the sewn seam allowance or trim with pinking shears.

## SEWING SLEEVES

Sewing sleeves to the garment is not difficult. Just take your time and refer to the following tips.

- Use lots of pins and keep the raw edges even.

- Start pinning the sleeve to the armhole at the side edges first; then work toward the shoulder point on both sides.

- Place the pins within the seam allowance, as close to the raw edge as possible.

- Sew as close to each pin as possible to keep the raw edges together. Stop with the needle down in the fabric when removing each pin.

- As you stop to remove a pin or to pivot, check that the bodice is not folded underneath in the small section you are about to sew.

- If you accidentally sew a little tuck in the fabric, use a seam ripper to remove only the stitches necessary to untuck the fabric. Resew just that small section.

## SEWING PLEATS

Pleats are marked with at least 2 lines: a fold line and a placement line. Transfer both markings from the pattern to the fabric pieces.

**1.** Mark the fabric with the pleat fold and placement lines.

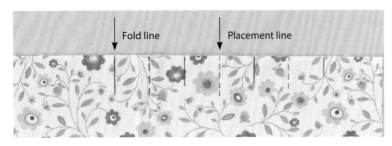

Fold line        Placement line

**2.** Pinch the fabric on the fold-line marking. Finger-press the very top edge of the fabric so the marking is directly on the crease of the fold.

**3.** Move the crease to the placement line so the 2 markings meet exactly and the raw edges at the top are even.

**4.** Press and pin the pleat. Make sure the fabric pleat is straight down the length of the fabric piece.

**5.** Repeat Steps 2–4 for all the pleats.

**6.** Baste across the pleat, sewing with the direction of the fold in the pleats.

## BACK CLOSURES

*The allowance for the center back opening on the projects is ⅜″ (1cm), which can accommodate hook-and-loop tape and other types of closures if you choose.*

Hook-and-loop tape is a common closure for doll clothes; it makes it easy for children to dress and undress their doll. Be sure to use the soft and flexible sew-on tape. If you can't find the ultrathin ⅜″-wide tape, trim the wider tape to size.

### Fully Open Back

Hem the garment before adding the hook-and-loop tape.

**1.** Finish the raw edges of the center back.

**2.** Fold one center back edge ⅜″ (1cm) to the wrong side and press. Leave the other edge unfolded.

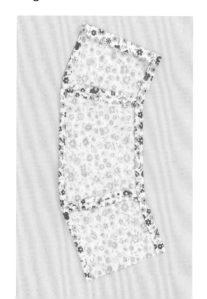

**3.** Cut the hook-and-loop tape to fit the back opening.

**4.** Sew the soft side of the tape to the inside of the folded edge, covering the raw edge.

**5.** Sew the scratchy side of the tape to the unfolded edge, onto the right side of the fabric.

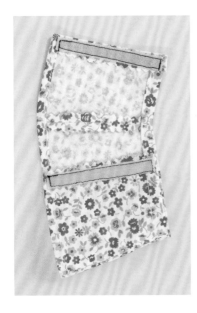

## Partially Open Back

Wait to hem the garment until the hook-and-loop tape is added.

**1.** Finish the raw edges of the center back.

**2.** Pin and sew the center back seam, right sides together, from the hem to 2″ (5.1cm) below the waist (or to the markings on the pattern), with a ⅜″ (1cm) seam allowance.

**3.** Press the seam allowances to one side. Keep the unsewn center back edges together and continue to press the opening up to the neckline. This will make one edge of the opening folded

and pressed to the wrong side, and the other edge will remain unfolded.

**4.** Sew the hook-and-loop tape to the opening by following Fully Open Back, Steps 3–5 (at left).

# Glossary

**BACKSTITCH (also called back tack)**
Sewing a few stitches back and forth at the beginning and end of seams secures the stitches and makes the seam more stable.

**BASTE (or basting stitch)** A long, straight stitch used to keep fabric or trim in place.

**CASING** A fabric tunnel that holds elastic or drawstrings, created by folding the fabric and then sewing the folded edge.

**CLIP THE CURVES** Clipping vertical cuts or cutting triangle notches in a curved seam allowance will allow the fabric more give.

**EDGESTITCH** A row of straight stitches sewn as close as possible to a folded edge or seam. They are sewn with the right side of the fabric facing up.

**FINGER-PRESS** To use the pressure of one's fingers and/or fingernails to flatten or make creases in the fabric instead of using an iron.

**INSEAM** The inside seam of a pant leg.

**NOTCHES** Markings on a pattern to indicate placement. Notches can be cut or marked.

**PIVOT** It's important to sew a corner in one continuous step. When you reach the corner, stop with the needle down in the fabric all the way; then raise the presser foot to turn the fabric.

**PLEATS** Folds that are pressed and sewn into a piece of fabric.

**RIGHT SIDES TOGETHER (or right sides facing together)** Fabrics are placed right sides together for sewing.

**SEAM** Sewing the edges of 2 pieces of fabrics together on a stitching line.

**SEAM ALLOWANCE** The distance from the stitching line to the raw edge of the fabric.

**SELVAGE** The lengthwise finished edges of a woven fabric.

**TOPSTITCH** A decorative, sometimes functional, row of stitches, often using contrasting thread, sewn next to an edge, a seam, or a fold.

**TIP** *Topstitching Doll Clothes*
Traditionally, topstitching is sewn ¼˝ (6mm) from the seam. However, for doll-sized projects, topstitch ⅛˝ (3mm) from the seam to maintain the proper scale. Using a clear presser foot helps when topstitching.

# Simple Skirts

These cute skirts are perfect projects for beginning sewists. View A is a basic straight skirt. View B has pleats in the front, giving it a gentle A-line silhouette.

A: SKILL LEVEL ●●
B: SKILL LEVEL ●●●

## MATERIALS

*Suggested fabrics: lightweight quilting cotton, fine-wale corduroy, lightweight denim, seersucker, chambray, or linen*

### Views A and B

SKIRT: Fat quarter (approximately 18″ × 22″/45.7 × 55.9cm)

HOOK-AND-LOOP TAPE (⅜″/1CM WIDE): ⅛ yard (11.4cm)

SEWING KIT (page 7)

## CUTTING

Use the patterns to cut out the fabric pieces (see Using a Pattern, page 11). Follow the cutting instructions on the patterns and use a fabric-marking tool to transfer any pattern markings onto the fabric pieces. For taller dolls, you may want to add ½″ to the length at the hem of these skirts.

### View A

- Simple Skirt Front 1
- Simple Skirt Back 2

### View B

- Pleated Skirt Front 3
- Pleated Skirt Back 4

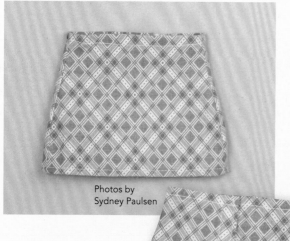

Photos by Sydney Paulsen

Photos by Sydney Paulsen

# SEWING INSTRUCTIONS

*All seam allowances are ¼˝ (6mm) and fabric is placed with right sides together, unless otherwise instructed.*

## Simple Skirt, View A

**1.** Pin and sew together the skirt front and skirt backs at the sides.

**2.** Finish the seam allowances; press them open or toward the back of the skirt.

**3.** Fold and press the top edge ¼˝ (6mm) toward the wrong side and press.

**4.** Fold again ¼˝ (6mm) toward the wrong side and press.

**5.** Sew across the folded fabric, sewing slowly over side seams and pleats if applicable.

> **Note** These skirts are designed to fit over the underwear that comes with the doll. If your doll isn't wearing underwear or has a smaller waist, increase the seam allowance at the side seams to ⅜˝ (1cm) or ½˝ (12mm).

**6.** Hem the lower edge (see Double-Fold Hem, page 16).

**7.** Make the center back opening (see Fully Open Back, page 22).

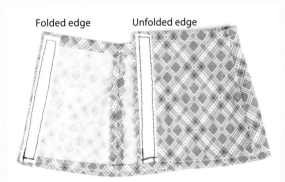

Folded edge     Unfolded edge

## Pleated Simple Skirt, View B

**1.** Fold and press the pleats (see Sewing Pleats, page 21).

**2.** Baste the pleats by sewing ¼″ (6mm) from the top raw edge.

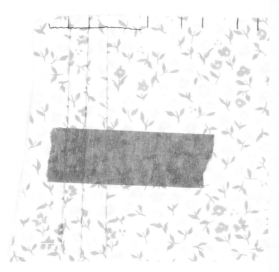

**TIP** After carefully folding and pressing the pleats, place a piece of tape across the pleated fabric. This helps when you are basting and secures the pleats while you finish the garment.

**3.** Follow Simple Skirt, View A, Steps 1–7 to finish this skirt.

## Embellishment Ideas

Add some extra details to give the pleated skirt a different look.

**1.** After basting the pleats, neatly edgestitch down the 2 center pleats with contrasting thread.

**2.** After the skirt is finished, sew tiny buttons to the center front.

# Twirl Skirts

Twirl skirts are always a crowd pleaser and a favorite of girls and their dolls. Dress them up with party shoes and lace, or create a playful look by pairing them with wellie boots or sneakers. Views A and B are great for those just learning to gather, and View C, with all those gathers, creates a half-circle skirt for the ultimate twirl.

**A:** SKILL LEVEL
**B:** SKILL LEVEL
**C:** SKILL LEVEL

A

B

C

## MATERIALS

*Suggested fabrics: quilting cotton, fine-wale corduroy, lightweight denim, seersucker, chambray, or linen*

### All views

WAISTBAND: Scrap of fabric

HOOK-AND-LOOP TAPE (⅜″/1CM WIDE): ⅛ yard (11.4cm)

SEWING KIT (page 7)

### View A

SKIRT: Fat quarter (approximately 18″ × 22″/45.7 × 55.9cm)

### View B

SKIRT: 3 coordinating fat quarters (approximately 18″ × 22″/45.7 × 55.9cm)

### View C

TOP TIER: Scrap of fabric

MIDDLE TIER: Fat quarter (approximately 18″ × 22″/45.7 × 55.9cm)

BOTTOM TIER: ⅛ yard (11.4cm) of fabric

## CUTTING

*Use the measurements provided to cut out the skirt pieces (see Cut Fabric Pieces Without Patterns, page 13).*

### All views

• Waistband: 1⅜″ × 7½″ (3.5 × 19.1cm) for each skirt

### View A

• Skirt: 4″ × 20″ (10.2 × 50.8cm)

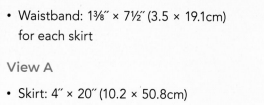

## View B

- Skirt top tier: 1⅝″ × 20″ (4.1 × 50.8cm)
- Skirt middle tier: 2¼″ × 20″ (5.7 × 50.8cm)
- Skirt bottom tier: 1½″ × 20″ (3.8 × 50.8cm)

## View C

- Skirt top tier: 1⅝″ × 11″ (4.1 × 27.9cm)
- Skirt middle tier: 2¾″ × 22″ (7 × 55.9cm)
- Skirt bottom tier: 2⅛″ × 40″ (5.4 × 101.6cm)

## SEWING INSTRUCTIONS

*All seam allowances are ¼″ (6mm) and fabric is placed with right sides together, unless otherwise instructed.*

### Twirl Skirt, View A

**1.** Hem the bottom of the skirt (see Double-Fold Hem, page 16).

**2.** Sew gathering stitches on the upper edge of the skirt piece and gather to fit the waistband piece (see Gathering, page 20).

**3.** Fold and press one long edge of the waistband piece ¼″ (6mm) to the wrong side.

**4.** Pin and sew the right side of the waistband's unfolded edge to the wrong side of the gathered skirt.

**5.** Fold the waistband to the right side of the skirt, and press. Edgestitch the waistband in place.

**6.** Sew the center back closure (see Fully Open Back, page 22).

## Twirl Skirt, View B

**1.** Pin and sew the 3 skirt tiers with right sides together. Finish and press the seam allowances toward the waist. Topstitch if desired.

**2.** Refer to Twirl Skirt, View A, Steps 1–6 to finish this skirt.

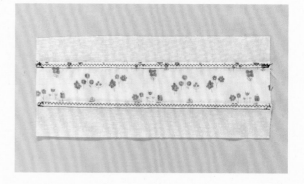

## Twirl Skirt, View C

**1.** Hem the lower edge of the bottom tier (see Double-Fold Hem, page 16).

**2.** Sew gathering stitches on the upper edges of the middle and bottom tiers (see Gathering, page 20). Gather the bottom tier to fit the lower edge of the middle tier. Gather the middle tier to fit the lower edge of the top tier.

**3.** Pin and sew the upper edge of the bottom tier to the lower edge of the middle tier. Pin and sew the upper edge of the middle tier to the lower edge of the top tier. Finish the seam allowances and press them up. Topstitch if desired.

**4.** Follow Twirl Skirt, View A, Steps 2–6 to finish this skirt.

# Simple Tops

This is a great beginner project. This fun top has the look of a T-shirt, but it's made with woven fabric instead of knit fabric. It's fully lined, which makes the neckline easier to sew as well.

A: SKILL LEVEL ● ◐
B: SKILL LEVEL ● ●

## MATERIALS

*Suggested fabrics: quilting cotton, poplin, lawn, seersucker, voile, lightweight chambray, Swiss Dot, or lightweight cotton*

TOP: Fat quarter (approximately 18″ × 22″/45.7 × 55.9cm)

LINING: Fat quarter (approximately 18″ × 22″/45.7 × 55.9cm)

HOOK-AND-LOOP TAPE (⅜″/1CM WIDE): ⅛ yard (11.4cm)

SEWING KIT (page 7)

## CUTTING

*Use the patterns to cut out the fabric and lining pieces (see Using a Pattern, page 11). Follow the cutting instructions on the patterns and use a fabric-marking tool to transfer any pattern markings onto the fabric pieces. Use the measurements provided to cut the remaining piece (see Cut Fabric Pieces Without Patterns, page 13).*

### View A

- Simple Top Front 5

- Simple Top Back 6

### View B

- Simple Top Front 5

- Simple Top Back 6

- Peplum: 2″ × 20″ (5.1 × 50.8cm)

# SEWING INSTRUCTIONS

*All seam allowances are ¼″ (6mm) and fabric is placed with right sides together, unless otherwise instructed.*

## Simple Top, View A

**1.** Pin and sew the front and back pieces together at the shoulders, with the raw edges even.

**2.** Press the seam allowances open.

**3.** Repeat Steps 1 and 2 for the lining front and lining back pieces.

**4.** Pin and sew the top to the lining at the neck and arm edges (see Sewing Curves, page 21). *Do not sew the center back edges.*

**5.** Turn the top right side out through the shoulder tunnels: Place a safety pin on the corner of the lining back and feed it between the 2 fabrics and through the shoulder. Repeat for the other side, pinning the safety pin to the other lining back.

**TIP** For additional help, watch my video tutorial about turning a lined bodice right side out; for the link, see Bonus Videos (page 112).

**6.** Press the top.

**7.** Pin and sew the top front to the top back and the lining front to the lining back at the sides, with right sides together. Press the seam allowances open.

**8.** Fold the lower edge of the top ¼˝ (6mm) to the wrong side and press. Repeat for the lining.

**9.** With the wrong sides of the fabrics together, sew across the folded edges, sewing through both fabrics.

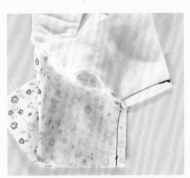

**10.** Sew the center back closure (see Fully Open Back, page 22).

## *Simple Peplum Top, View B*

**1.** Follow Simple Top, View A, Steps 1–7.

**2.** Baste the lining and shirt together at the lower edges.

**3.** Hem the lower edge of the peplum piece (see Double-Fold Hem, page 16).

**4.** Sew gathering stitches on the top edge and gather to fit the lower edge of the top (see Gathering, page 20).

**5.** Pin and sew the peplum piece to the shirt. Finish the seam allowances and press them up toward the shirt. Topstitch.

**6.** Sew the center back closure (see Fully Open Back, page 22).

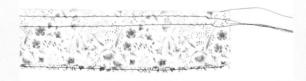

# Swing Tank Tops

A: SKILL LEVEL ●● ◐
B: SKILL LEVEL ●● ○
C: SKILL LEVEL ●● ◐
D: SKILL LEVEL ●● ○

This playful top is another great beginner project. Using a very lightweight fabric results in a softer drape. The mock placket gives it more of a tailored appearance, and extending the straps for View D turns the top into an adorable jumper.

## MATERIALS

*Suggested fabrics: quilting cotton, poplin, Swiss Dot, seersucker, lawn, or voile*

### All views

TOP AND STRAPS: Fat quarter (approximately 18″ × 22″/45.7 × 55.9cm)

LINING: Small scrap of lightweight cotton fabric

ELASTIC (¼″/6MM WIDE): 3″ (7.6cm)

HOOK-AND-LOOP TAPE (⅜″/1CM WIDE): Small scrap

SEWING KIT (page 7)

### Views B and D

BUTTONS, ¼″ (6 MM): 5

## CUTTING

Use the patterns to cut out the fabric and lining pieces (see Using a Pattern, page 11). Follow the cutting instructions on the patterns and use a fabric-marking tool to transfer any pattern markings onto the fabric pieces.

### All views

- Swing Tank Top Front 7
- Swing Tank Top Back 8
- Swing Tank Top Facing 9
- Swing Tank Top Strap 10

View A

View B

**View C**

**View D**

Photos by
Sydney Paulsen

Photos by
Sydney Paulsen

## SEWING INSTRUCTIONS

*All seam allowances are ¼˝ (6mm) and fabric is placed with right sides together, unless otherwise instructed.*

### Swing Top, Views A and C

*Fasten the straps at the back, either straight or crossed for alternate views.*

**Make the Straps and Front**

**1.** Transfer the strap placement markings to the right side of the top front and top back.

**2.** Make 2 straps with one finished end each (see Make Straps, page 19).

**3.** Pin and baste the unfinished end of each strap to the front at the markings, with right sides together.

**4.** Pin and sew the facing to the front along the top edge only (see Sewing Curves, page 21).

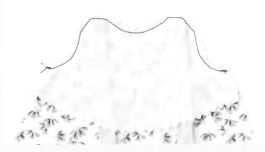

**5.** Cut diagonally at the corners and cut triangle-shaped notches within the seam allowances. Turn the front right side out and press.

**6.** Cut 2 pieces of hook-and-loop tape 1″ (2.5cm) long. Sew the loop side of the tape on the *right side* of the strap ends; sew a small square shape at the very end and then trim to ¼″ (6mm).

**TIP** It's easier to sew a larger piece of hook-and-loop tape in place than the smaller pieces that are often needed for doll clothes.

## Make the Back

**1.** Make a casing on the top edge (see Sew a Casing for Elastic, page 18), but with the first fold ¼″ (6mm) and the second fold ½″ (12mm).

**2.** Sew the hook side of the hook-and-loop tape to the back at the markings, sewing only at the top and bottom edges of the casing so the elastic can still be inserted.

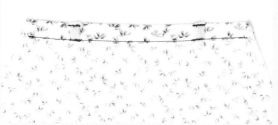

**3.** Use a bodkin or safety pin to insert the elastic inside the casing. With a 3″ (7.6cm) length of elastic, use 2 safety pins and place a safety pin on each end of the elastic.

**TIP** You can use a longer length of elastic if you find it easier to work with; just remember to mark and trim it to the recommended length before sewing the ends.

**4.** Secure the elastic by sewing across the casing and the elastic.

**5.** Pin and sew the back to the front at the side edges, aligning the top, bottom, and side edges. Finish the edges of the seam allowances.

## Make the Hem

Hem the bottom edge (see Double-Fold Hem, page 16).

## *Swing Top, Views B and D*

*Note that the straps are longer for View D than for the other swing tops.*

## Mock Placket in Top Front

**1.** Fold the front piece in half, with wrong sides together, and lightly press.

**2.** Sew ⅜″ (1cm) from the center fold.

**3.** Open the front piece and press the fold flat. Edgestitch on both sides to create the mock placket.

**TIP** Slide a narrow wooden knitting needle into the mock placket and press to first remove the crease; remove the knitting needle and then press flat.

### Make the Straps, Top Front, and Top Back

**1.** Follow Swing Top, Views A and C; Make the Straps and Front; Steps 1–5.

**2.** Follow Swing Top, Views A and C; Make the Back; Steps 1–5.

**3.** Hem the bottom edge (see Double-Fold Hem, page 16).

**4.** Sew the buttons along the mock placket on the front.

# Raglan Tops

These easy-fitting tops are a great project for intermediate beginners. Fold and sew the casings carefully—especially the neckline. Work one section at a time as you press and as you sew. Beginners might want to start with View A or B. To make View B easier to sew, just eliminate the waistline casing and simply hem the bottom edge.

A: SKILL LEVEL
B: SKILL LEVEL
C: SKILL LEVEL

## MATERIALS

*Suggested fabrics: quilting cotton, poplin, lawn, voile, Swiss Dot, lightweight cotton, or chambray*

### All views

TOP: Fat quarter (approximately 18″ × 22″/45.7 × 55.9cm)

ELASTIC (⅛″/3MM WIDE): ⅓ yard (30.5cm)

SEWING KIT (page 7)

### View B

ELASTIC (⅛″/3MM WIDE): Additional 6″ (15.2cm) for waistband casing

### View C

BUTTONS (⅛″–¼″/3–6MM): 4

## CUTTING

*Use the patterns to cut out the fabric pieces (see Using a Pattern, page 11). Follow the cutting instructions on the patterns and use a fabric-marking tool to transfer any pattern markings onto the fabric pieces.*

### All views

- Raglan Top Front 11
- Raglan Top Back 12
- Raglan Sleeve 13

### View A

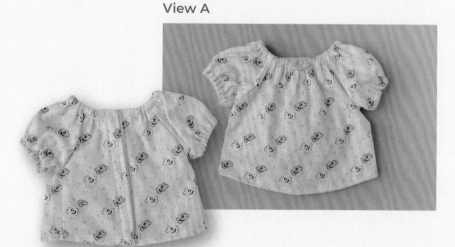

**View B**

**View C**

## SEWING INSTRUCTIONS

*All seam allowances are ¼″ (6mm) and fabric is placed with right sides together, unless otherwise instructed.*

### Raglan Top, View A

**1.** Make a casing on the lower edges of both sleeves, with both folds ¼″ (6mm) wide (see Sew a Casing for Elastic, page 18).

**2.** Pin and sew each sleeve to a back piece. Finish and press the seam allowances.

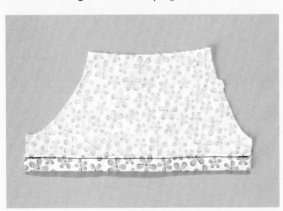

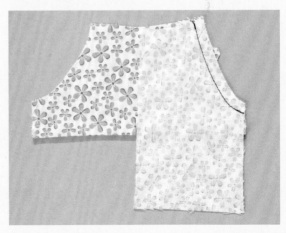

**3.** Pin and sew the sleeves to the bodice front. Finish and press the seam allowances.

**4.** Make a casing on the top edge, with both folds ¼″ (6mm) wide. Stop and start stitching at the pattern markings.

**5.** Insert a 3″ (7.6cm)-long piece of elastic into the sleeve casings. Secure the elastic by sewing across the casing and the elastic.

**6.** Pin and sew the side and sleeve seams in one continuous step, pivoting at the sleeve/shirt seam.

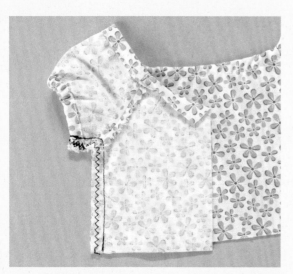

**7.** Insert 5½″–6″ (14–16.2cm) of elastic through the neckline casing. Secure the elastic by sewing across the casing and the elastic at the markings. Sew the remainder of the casing, from the opening to the center back, to finish.

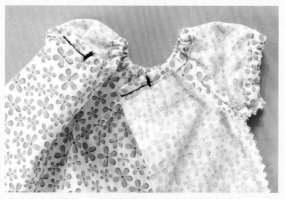

**TIP** *Sewing Small*

If you don't have a safety pin small enough to easily fit inside the casing, try using a bodkin or large tapestry needle that has a blunt end. Cut the elastic longer than needed, but mark the measurement needed. The needle easily glides through the casing.

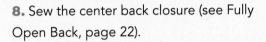

**8.** Sew the center back closure (see Fully Open Back, page 22).

**9.** Sew a double-fold hem (see Double-Fold Hem, page 16).

## *Raglan Top with Waist Elastic, View B*

**1.** Follow Raglan Top, View A, Steps 1–7 (pages 47 and 48).

**2.** Make a waistband casing at the lower edge of the top, with both folds ¼″ (6mm) wide. Stop and start stitching at the pattern markings.

**3.** Insert 6″ (16.2cm) of elastic. Secure the elastic by sewing across the casing and the elastic. Sew the remainder of the casing.

**4.** Sew the center back closure (see Fully Open Back, page 22).

## *Raglan Top with Mock Placket, View C*

**1.** Fold the front piece in half with wrong sides together. Lightly press.

**2.** Sew ⅜″ (1cm) from the center fold.

**3.** Open the front piece and press the fold flat. Edgestitch on both sides to create the mock placket.

**4.** Follow Raglan Top, View A, Steps 1–9 (pages 47–49).

**5.** Sew the buttons on the mock placket.

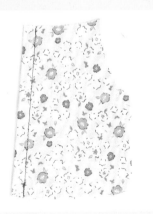

# Simple Shorts and Pants

These easy-fitting bottoms are easy to sew and a great wardrobe builder. The weight of the fabric affects the fit and look. Choose a lightweight fabric for a softer drape and a heavier-weight fabric, such as twill or denim, for a more structured/tailored appearance. Remove the mock placket for an easier project.

**A:** SKILL LEVEL
**B:** SKILL LEVEL
**C:** SKILL LEVEL

## MATERIALS

*Suggested fabrics: quilting cotton, lightweight denim or twill, chambray, or linen*

**All views**

PANTS/SHORTS: Fat quarter (approximately 18″ × 22″/45.7 × 55.9cm)

ELASTIC (¼″/6MM WIDE): ¼ yard (22.9cm)

SEWING KIT (page 7)

**View A**

TRIM (¼″/6MM WIDE): ¼ yard (22.9cm) for hem

**View C**

POCKETS: Scraps of fabric

## CUTTING

*Use the patterns to cut out the fabric pieces (see Using a Pattern, page 11). Follow the cutting instructions on the patterns and use a fabric-marking tool to transfer any pattern markings onto the fabric pieces. Transfer the mock fly-stitching lines and pocket placement markings onto the right side of the pant pieces.*

**All views**

• Simple Shorts and Pants 14

View A

View B

## View C

- Cargo Pants Pocket 15
- Cargo Pants Pocket Lining 16
- Cargo Pants Pocket Flap 17
- See Bonus Design: Cropped Cargo Pants (page 55) for contrast fabric requirements.

## SEWING INSTRUCTIONS

*All seam allowances are ¼˝ (6mm) and fabric is placed with right sides together, unless otherwise instructed.*

### Shorts, View A, and Pants, View B

**1.** Hem the bottom edges (see Double-Fold Hem, page 16).

**2.** For the shorts only, sew lace to the finished hem so the decorative edge peeks out below the hem.

**3.** Pin and sew the 2 leg pieces together at the center front. Finish the seam allowances and press them to one side.

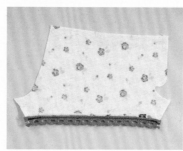

**4.** With the right side facing up, sew the mock fly detail.

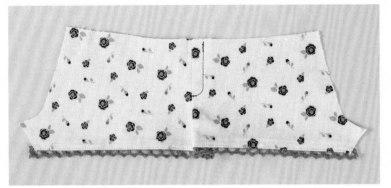

**5.** Fold and press the waist edge ¼″ (6mm) to the wrong side. Fold again ⅜″ (1cm) to the wrong side and press. *Don't sew it yet.*

**6.** Unfold the waist edge and sew the center back seam. Finish the seam allowances.

**7.** Refold and press the waist edge to make a casing.

**8.** Sew across the folded fabric, leaving a small opening for the elastic insertion.

**TIP** When the project won't fit or loop over the free arm of the machine, work with the project right side out. Place it under the needle with the wrong side of the fabric under the presser foot. Keep the bulk of the project out of the way with your left hand. Sew slowly and sew a little section at a time, stopping to reposition your hands or adjust the project.

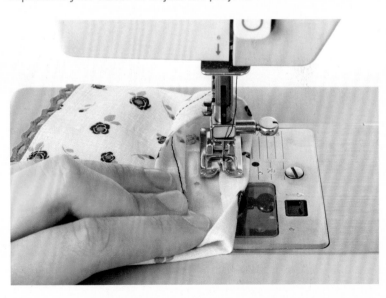

**9.** Pin and sew the inseam, keeping the crotch seam matched and the hems even. Finish the seam allowances.

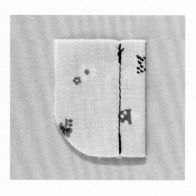

**10.** Insert the elastic into the opening in the casing. Once the elastic is back to the opening, sew the ends of the elastic together. If needed, pull on both ends and pull out some extra slack, making sure the elastic is not twisted.

**11.** Sew the opening closed.

*Pants with Cargo Pockets, View C*

**1.** Fold the pocket piece in half, wrong sides together, and sew ⅜″ (1cm) from the fold.

**2.** Open the fabric and press the mock placket flat.

**3.** Fold the top edge of the pocket and the pocket lining ⅜″ (1cm) to the wrong side and press. Topstitch the top edge.

**4.** Pin and sew the pocket piece to the pocket lining at the sides and bottom edge. Trim the seam allowances to ⅛″ (3mm) and turn right side out. Press.

**5.** Sew the top edge.

**6.** Repeat Step 4 for the flap and flap lining pieces. Finish the raw edges of the flap piece.

**7.** Pin and sew the pocket to the pants pieces at the markings. Pin and sew the flaps to the pants directly above the pockets, with the raw edge of the flap located where indicated on the pattern.

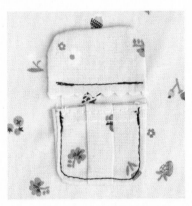

**8.** Fold and press the flap down. Sew the top edge of the flap.

**9.** Follow Shorts, View A, and Pants, View B, Steps 1 and 3–11 to finish this project.

# Bonus Design ♥ CROPPED CARGO PANTS

To view these pants on a doll, see Raglan Tops (page 45).

**Contrast Hems**

**1.** Cut the pants pattern piece along the shorter cutting line.

**2.** Cut 2 pieces 1⅜″ × 4″ (3.5 × 10.2cm) for the cuffs.

**3.** Fold and press one long edge of each cuff ¼″ (6mm) to the wrong side.

**4.** Pin and sew the unfolded edge of the cuffs to the lower edge of the pant-legs bottom, with the right side of the cuff facing the wrong side of the pant-leg bottom.

**5.** Fold the cuff to the right side of the pant-leg bottom, enclosing all the raw edges. Pin and sew the cuff to the pant-leg bottom. (See Vintage Party Dress, View C, Sleeves, page 82, for more detailed information.)

### Contrast Fabric Pockets

*Use Pocket Lining 16 and Pocket Flap 17.*

To make 2 pockets:

- From the main fabric, cut 4 pocket lining pieces (16) and 2 flaps (17).

- From the contrast fabric, cut 2 flaps (17) and 1 strip of fabric ⅞″ × 3¼″.

**1.** Fold and press the long edges of the fabric strip ¼″ (6mm) to the wrong side. Cut into 2 pieces.

**2.** Sew the strips to the center of 2 pocket lining pieces.

**3.** Fold the top edge of both pocket linings ¼″ (6mm) to the wrong side and press.

**4.** Pin and sew the pocket linings with right sides together at the sides and bottom edge. Trim the seam allowances to ⅛″ (3mm) and turn right side out. Press.

**5.** Sew the top edge.

**6.** Pin and sew the flap pieces (one main fabric and one contrast fabric) with right sides together along the sides and bottom edge. Trim the seam allowances to ⅛″ (3mm) and turn right side out. Press. Finish the open straight edge.

**7.** Follow Pants with Cargo Pockets, View C, Steps 7–9 to finish this project.

# Sundresses

This is a great design to start with when you want to learn how to sew dresses. The lined bodice is slightly less complicated than the classic sleeveless dress and the dresses with sleeves.

A: SKILL LEVEL
B: SKILL LEVEL
C: SKILL LEVEL
D: SKILL LEVEL

## MATERIALS

*Suggested fabrics: lightweight quilting cotton, poplin, broadcloth, lawn, seersucker, eyelet, chambray, or linen*

### All views

BODICE, SKIRT, AND STRAPS (VIEWS C AND D ONLY): Fat quarter (approximately 18″ × 22″/45.7 × 55.9cm)

LINING: Large scrap of fabric, at least 4″ × 12″ (10.2 × 30.5cm)

HOOK-AND-LOOP TAPE (⅜″/1CM WIDE): ⅛ yard (11.4cm)

SEWING KIT (page 7)

### View A

CONTRASTING STRAPS: Large scrap of fabric, at least 7″ (17.8 cm) square

### View B

RIBBON (⅜″/1CM WIDE): 5″ (12.7cm)

WAISTBAND AND CONTRASTING STRAPS: Large scrap of fabric at least 1½″ × 8″ (3.8 × 20.3cm)

### View C

BODICE ACCENT: Small scrap of fabric

RIBBON (⅛″/3MM WIDE): 5″ (12.7cm)

### View D

WAISTBAND AND COLLARS: Large scrap of fabric at least 4″ × 8″ (10.2 × 20.3cm)

BUTTONS (¼″/6MM): 2

## CUTTING

*Use the patterns to cut out the fabric and lining pieces (see Using a Pattern, page 11). Transfer all markings from the patterns to the fabric pieces.*

### All views

- Sundress Bodice Front 21
- Sundress Bodice Back 22
- Sundress Strap 23

## View A

- Sundress Skirt 24

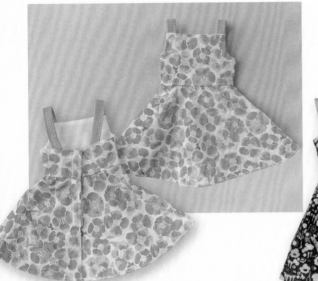

## View B

- Waistband: 1″ × 7⅜″ (2.5 × 18.7cm)
- Skirt piece: 5″ × 21″ (12.7 × 53.3cm)

Photos by Sydney Paulsen

## View C

- Sundress Skirt 24
- Sundress Bodice Front Accent 26

## View D

- Sundress Collar 25
- Waistband: 1″ × 7⅜″ (2.5 × 18.7cm)
- Skirt piece: 5″ × 21″ (12.7 × 53.3cm)

Photos by Sydney Paulsen

# SEWING INSTRUCTIONS

*All seam allowances are ¼˝ (6mm) and fabric is placed with right sides together, unless otherwise instructed.*

## Sundress, View A

### Bodice and Straps

**1.** Pin and sew together the bodice front and bodice back pieces at the sides.

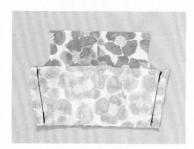

**2.** Press the seam allowances open (see Press Seam Allowances, page 15).

**TIP** Pressing well throughout construction will make your project go together much more easily, and it will always make your sewing projects look much better than when the pressing steps are skipped.

**3.** Repeat Steps 1 and 2 for the lining front and lining back pieces.

**4.** Fold, press, and sew the strap piece without finished ends (see Make Straps, page 19). Cut into 2 pieces, each 3½˝ (8.9cm) long.

**5.** Pin and baste the straps to the right side of the bodice front at the markings.

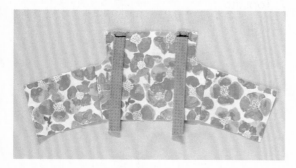

**6.** Pin the lining to the bodice at the upper edge, keeping all edges even.

**7.** Sew the lining to the bodice between the dot markings on the bodice back pieces.

**TIP** Use a short stitch length (1.5–2.0mm) to sew curves.

**8.** Trim the seam allowances by cutting diagonally at the corners. Cut small triangle-shaped notches along the curved seams or trim with pinking shears, taking care not to cut the stitches.

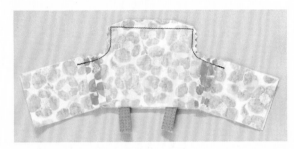

**9.** Turn the bodice right side out and use a corner-turning tool to shape the corners. Press.

**11.** Insert the loose ends of the straps ¼″ (6mm) between the bodice and lining back pieces at the markings. Sew the top edges together, close to the folded edge.

**TIP** The strap length may need adjusting for different dolls. Place the bodice on your doll before sewing the strap ends to the bodice back to make a custom fit.

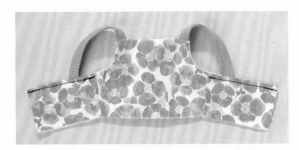

**12.** Baste together the bodice and lining pieces along the lower and center back edges.

**10.** Fold the open top edges of the bodice and lining back pieces ¼″ (6mm) to the wrong side and press.

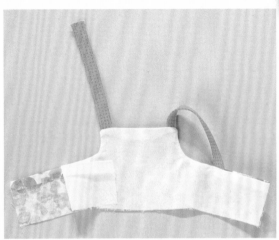

### Skirt

**1.** Pin and sew the skirt piece to the bodice.

**2.** Finish the seam allowances and press them up toward the bodice.

**3.** Topstitch along the lower edge of the bodice.

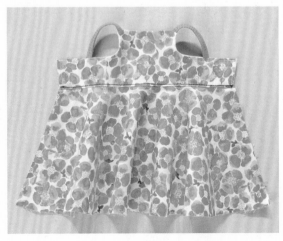

### Finish

**1.** Sew the center back seam and closure (see Partially Open Back, page 23).

**2.** Hem the skirt (see Hem a Curved Edge / Narrow Hem, page 17).

---

### Sundress, View B

**1.** Follow Sundress, View A; Bodice and Straps; Steps 1–3.

**2.** Pin and sew the waistband to the lower edge of the bodice. Finish the seam allowances.

**3.** Sew gathering stitches on the top edge of the skirt piece and gather to fit the waistband (see Gathering, page 20).

**4.** Pin and sew the skirt piece to the waistband using a ⅜″ (1cm) seam allowance.

**TIP** Lightly press the waistband seam allowances up toward the bodice to keep them out of the way while sewing the skirt piece to the waistband.

**5.** Finish the seam allowances and press all seam allowances toward the waistband.

**6.** Follow Sundress, View A; Finish; Steps 1 and 2.

**7.** Tie the ribbon into a bow, trim any extra ribbon from the ends, and hand sew it to the waistband.

## Sundress, View C

### Bodice Detail

**1.** Sew the bottom edge of the accent piece ¼˝ (6mm) from the raw edge, using a short stitch length (1.5).

**2.** Cut small triangle notches on the curved raw edge, or trim it with pinking shears. Press the curved edge ¼˝ (6mm) to the wrong side of the fabric. The stitching line makes this easier to do. As you fold and press, keep the crease of the fold directly on the stitches.

**3.** Pin the accent piece to the right side of the bodice front, with both right sides facing up, and sew along the folded edge. Carefully trim the accent piece to match the bodice at the side and top edges.

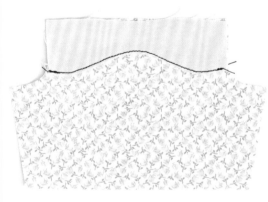

### Finish

**1.** Follow all the steps for Sundress, View A.

**2.** Tie the ribbon into a bow, trim any extra ribbon from the ends, and hand sew it to the center front of the dress.

## Sundress, View D

### Collar

**1.** Pin and sew the collar pieces to the collar lining pieces, leaving the top edge unsewn.

**2.** Trim the seam allowances to ⅛″ (3mm) and trim diagonally at the corners.

**3.** Turn the collar pieces right side out and use a corner-turning tool to poke out the corners. Press.

**4.** Pin and baste the collars to the right side of the bodice, with the collars meeting at the center front.

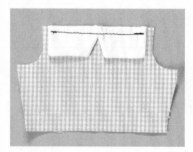

**TIP** Use Wonder Tape or fabric glue to hold the collars in place. It's easier than using pins.

### Finish

**1.** Follow Sundress, View B, Steps 1–6.

**2.** Sew the buttons to the bodice front.

**3.** Hand sew the collar to keep it from flipping up. Work from the inside of the dress, sewing only through the lining side of the collar, so the stitches do not show on the outside of the dress.

# Bonus Designs 🖤

**Turn the Dress into a Summer Top**

To make this cute summer top, use the patterns and follow the steps for Sundress, View B.

- Cut the skirt piece 2½˝ × 19˝ (6.4 × 48.3cm).

- Omit the waistband; just gather the skirt and sew it to the bottom of the bodice.

- Sew ¼˝ (6mm) picot trim to the finished hem.

- Buttons are a great way to add more detail and interest. Sew ⅜˝ (10mm) buttons on the bodice back, just below the straps. Buttons would also look great sewn to the bodice front.

**Add Trim for a Vintage Picnic Sundress**

*You'll need 1½ yards of rickrack trim.*

**1.** Use the patterns and follow the instructions for Sundress, View A, Steps 1–12.

**2.** Cut the skirt pieces as follows:

Lower skirt piece: 1⅝″ × 21″ (4.1 × 53.3cm)

Upper skirt piece: 3¾″ × 21″ (9.5 × 53.3cm)

**3.** Before sewing the skirt to the finished bodice, sew rickrack to the right side of the bodice. Use a seam gauge and Wonder Tape (or fabric glue) to align the rickrack, instead of using pins, so the center of the rickrack is ⅜″ (1cm) from the lower edge of the bodice. Baste the rickrack in place.

**TIP** Before sewing the rickrack to the fabric, seal the ends with anti-fray sealant, to prevent it from unraveling.

**4.** Align a 22″ (56cm) length of rickrack on the right side of the lower skirt piece's top edge so the center of the rickrack is ¼″ (6mm) from the raw edge. Stitch it in place through the center of the rickrack.

**5.** Sew the 2 skirt pieces together with the rickrack sandwiched in the middle. Finish the seam allowances and press them toward the bodice.

**6.** Sew gathering stitches on the top edge of the skirt piece and gather to fit the bodice (see Gathering, page 20). Sew the bodice to the skirt. Finish the seam allowances and press them toward the bodice.

**7.** Follow Sundress, View A; Finish; Steps 1 and 2.

**8.** After hemming the dress, sew rickrack to the inside on the finished hem so it peeks out beyond the hem.

# Classic Sleeveless Dress

This classic dress design has stood the test of time. The skirt design of Views A, C, and D gives this traditional dress clean lines and a modern style, and View B has a very full skirt for a pretty silhouette.

**A:** SKILL LEVEL
**B:** SKILL LEVEL

67

**TIP** *Beginner's Hem*
The curved hemline on this dress is tricky and little time consuming.
Adding unfinished lace, such as the eyelet lace on View A and View D,
makes this skirt style easier to hem.

**C:** SKILL LEVEL ⊙⊙⊙⊙⊙
**D:** SKILL LEVEL ⊙⊙⊙⊙⊙

Photo by Page + Pixel

## MATERIALS

*Suggested fabrics: lightweight quilting cotton, poplin, chambray, or broadcloth*

### All views

HOOK-AND-LOOP TAPE
(⅜"/1CM WIDE): ⅛ yard (11.4cm)

SEWING KIT (page 7)

### View A

DRESS AND LINING:
Fat quarter (approximately
18" × 22"/45.7 × 55.9cm)

LACE/TRIM (¼"–½"/6–12MM WIDE):
⅔ yard (61cm)

### View B

DRESS AND LINING:
Fat quarter (approximately
18" × 22"/45.7 × 55.9cm)

RIBBON (⅜"/1CM WIDE) FOR SASH:
⅔ yard (61cm)

### View C

DRESS AND LINING:
Fat quarter (approximately
18" × 22"/45.7 × 55.9cm)

RIBBON (⅛"/3MM WIDE): Scrap

### View D

BODICE AND LINING:
Fat quarter (approximately
18" × 22"/45.7 × 55.9cm)

SKIRT: Fat quarter (approximately
18" × 22"/45.7 × 55.9cm)

LACE/TRIM (¼"–½"/6–12MM WIDE):
⅔ yard (61cm)

BUTTONS (³⁄₁₆"/5MM): 4

## CUTTING

*Use the patterns to cut out the fabric and lining pieces (see Using a Pattern, page 11). Follow the cutting instructions on the patterns and use a fabric-marking tool to transfer any pattern markings onto the fabric pieces.*

### All Views

- Classic Sleeveless Dress Bodice Front 27 (For View D, see sewing instructions before cutting.)
- Classic Sleeveless Dress Bodice Back 28

## Views A

- Classic Sleeveless Dress Skirt 29

## View B

- Skirt: 5⅛″ × 20″ (13 × 50.8cm)

## View C

- Classic Sleeveless Dress Skirt 29

## View D

- Classic Sleeveless Dress Skirt 29

- Classic Sleeveless Dress Bodice Front 27
  (Cut 1 for lining.)

  Cut a piece 4½″ × 9″ (11.4 × 22.9cm). See
  the sewing instructions for the front pintuck
  detail.

- Classic Sleeveless Dress Collar 30

# SEWING INSTRUCTIONS

*All seam allowances are ¼″ (6mm) and fabric is placed with right sides together, unless otherwise instructed.*

## Classic Sleeveless Dress, Views A and C

**1.** Sew the bodice front to the bodice back pieces at the shoulders. Press the seam allowances open.

**2.** Repeat Step 1 for the lining.

**3.** Sew the lining to the bodice at the neck and arm openings. Cut triangle notches in the curved seam allowances, or trim with pinking shears.

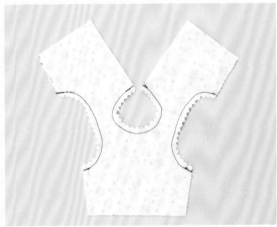

**4.** Turn the bodice right side out through the shoulder tunnels by placing a safety pin on the corner of the back lining piece and feeding it between the fabrics at the shoulder. Repeat for the other side. Press. (See Simple Top, View A, Step 5, page 36.)

**5.** Press open the underarm seam allowances. Pin and sew the side seams, sewing the lining front to the lining back and the bodice front to the bodice back at the side edges with one continuous seam.

**6.** Press the side seam allowances open.

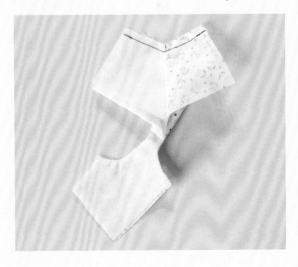

**7.** Press the bodice and baste the bottom raw edges together just inside the ¼″ (6mm) seam allowance.

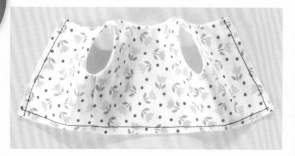

**8.** Pin and sew the skirt piece to the bodice. Finish the seam allowances and press them toward the bodice. Topstitch.

**9.** Sew the center back seam and closure (see Partially Open Back, page 23).

**10. VIEW A:** Hem the dress with lace (see Hem with Trims, page 17).

**VIEW C:** Sew the hem (see Double-Fold Hem, page 16). Tie the ribbon into a bow and sew it to the bodice front.

## Classic Sleeveless Dress, View B

**1.** Follow Classic Sleeveless Dress, View A, Steps 1–7 to make the bodice.

**2.** Sew gathering stitches on the upper edge of the skirt piece and gather the skirt to fit the lower edge of the bodice (see Gathering, page 20).

**3.** Sew the center back seam and closure (see Partially Open Back, page 23).

**4.** Hem the dress (see Double-Fold Hem, page 16).

**5.** Sew, or simply tie, a ribbon to the waist.

## Classic Sleeveless Dress, View D

**1.** Use a ruler and fabric marker to mark the folds for the 4 pintucks. Fold the fabric in half and mark the center point. Measure and mark ¼″ (6mm) and ¾″ (1.9cm) from the center on both sides and on both the top and bottom edges of the fabric.

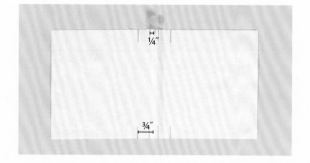

**2.** Pinch and finger-press a crease on each fold line. Fold the length of the fabric and press each fold, keeping the raw edges at the top and bottom even. Use just the edge of the iron to avoid unpressing the other folds.

**3.** Sew ⅛″ (3mm) from the fold to make each pintuck. Press the pintucks away from the center.

**4.** Fold the fabric in half at the center mark so the pintucks are equal distance from the center. Place the bodice front pattern on the fold to cut out the bodice front. Baste the pintucks at the top and bottom edges.

**5.** Sew the bodice front to the bodice back pieces at the shoulders. Press the seam allowances open. Repeat with the lining pieces.

**6.** Sew 2 collar pieces together at the outer edges, leaving the neck edge unsewn. Repeat for the other 2 collar pieces.

**7.** Trim the seam allowances to ⅛″ (3mm) and turn them right side out. Press. Use a corner-turning tool to smooth out the curves as you press.

**8.** Pin and baste the collars to the right side of the bodice, with the collars meeting at the center front.

**9.** Follow Classic Sleeveless Dress, View A, Steps 3–7 to complete the bodice.

**10.** Pin and sew the skirt piece to the bodice. Finish the seam allowances and press them toward the bodice. Topstitch.

**11.** Sew the center back seam and closure (see Partially Open Back, page 23).

**12.** Hem the dress with lace (see Hem with Trims, page 17).

**13.** Sew the buttons at the center front.

# Vintage Party Dress

Inspired by vintage children's books, these dresses are sweet and timeless. There are three different sleeve finishes, two collar choices, and the option to add a center front mock placket to create the look of a shirt dress.

A: SKILL LEVEL ⊙⊙⊙
B: SKILL LEVEL ⊙⊙⊙
C: SKILL LEVEL ⊙⊙⊙⊙

## MATERIALS

*Suggested fabrics: quilting cotton, piqué, or chambray*

### All views

DRESS: Fat quarter (approximately 18″ × 22″/45.7 × 55.9cm)

LINING: Lightweight cotton, 5″ × 12″ (12.7 × 30.5cm)

ELASTIC (⅛″/3MM WIDE): ¼ yard (22.9cm)

SEWING KIT (page 7)

### Views B and C

COLLAR AND SLEEVE BAND/BINDING: Large scrap of fabric

### View C

BUTTONS (³⁄₁₆″/5MM): 6

RIBBON (⅜″/1CM WIDE): ⅔ yard (61cm) for sash

## CUTTING

Use the patterns to cut out the fabric and lining pieces (see Using a Pattern, page 11). Follow the cutting instructions on the patterns and use a fabric-marking tool to transfer any pattern markings onto the fabric pieces. Use the measurements provided to cut out the remaining pieces (Cut Fabric Pieces Without Patterns, page 13). For taller dolls, you may want to use the longer length skirt (View B) when making these dresses.

### All views

- Vintage Party Dress Bodice Front 31
- Vintage Party Dress Bodice Back 32
- Vintage Party Dress Sleeve 33

### View A

- Skirt: 4¾″ × 20″ (12.1 × 50.8cm)

## View B

- Skirt: 5¼″ × 20″ (13.3 × 50.8cm)
- Sleeve bands: 1⅜″ × 3¾″ (3.5 × 9.5cm); cut 2.
- Vintage Party Dress Collar 34

## View C

- Skirt: 4¾″ × 20″ (12.1 × 50.8cm)
- Sleeve binding: 1¼″ × 3¾″ (3.2 × 9.5cm); cut 2.
- Vintage Party Dress Collar 35

## SEWING INSTRUCTIONS

*All seam allowances are ¼″ (6mm) and fabric is placed with right sides together, unless otherwise instructed. Note that the sleeve finishes are done after the sleeves are sewn to the bodice but the instructional photos show the sleeves separately so it is easier to see the techniques.*

## Vintage Party Dress, View A

### Bodice

**1.** Pin and sew the bodice front to the bodice back at the shoulders. Press the seam allowances open.

**2.** Repeat Step 1 for the lining front and lining back pieces.

**3.** Pin and sew the bodice to the bodice lining at the neckline (see Sewing Curves, page 21). Cut triangle-shaped notches within the curved seam allowances.

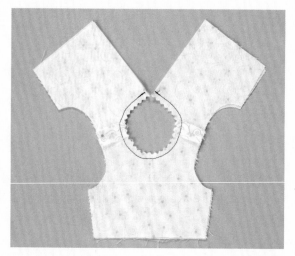

**4.** Turn the bodice right side out and press. Baste all the *raw* edges just inside the ¼˝ (6mm) seam allowance, sewing through both the bodice and the lining.

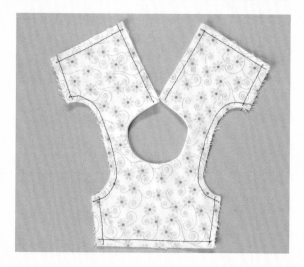

## Sleeves

**1.** Fold and press the lower edge ¼″ (6mm) twice to the wrong side, pressing after each fold.

**2.** Sew close to the inside folded edge.

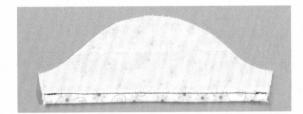

**3.** Sew gathering stitches on the curved edge of the sleeves and gather to fit the bodice (see Gathering, page 20).

**4.** Pin and sew the sleeves to the bodice, concentrating the gathers at the top of the curve (see Sewing Sleeves, page 21). Finish the seam allowances.

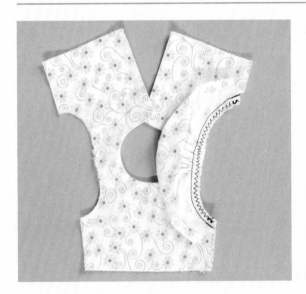

**5.** Insert 3″ (7.6cm) of elastic into the sleeve casings. Secure the elastic by sewing across the casing and the elastic. Photo shows the elastic detail only; the sleeve should be sewn to the bodice first.

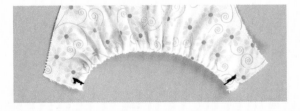

## Finish

**1.** Pin and sew the sleeve and side seams in one continuous step, keeping the sleeve hems even. Finish the seam allowances and press toward the back.

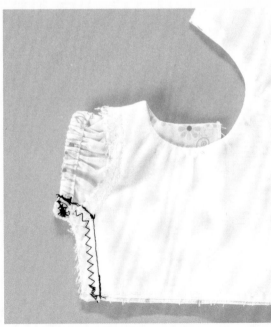

**2.** Sew gathering stitches on the upper edge of the skirt and gather it to fit the bodice (see Gathering, page 20).

**3.** Pin and sew the skirt piece to the bodice. Finish the seam allowances and press them toward the bodice. Topstitch.

**4.** Sew the center back seam and closure (see Partially Open Back, page 23).

**5.** Hem the dress (see Double-Fold Hem, page 16).

## Vintage Party Dress, View B

### Bodice and Collar

**1.** Pin and sew the bodice front to the bodice back at the shoulders. Press the seam allowances open.

**2.** Repeat Step 1 for the lining front and lining back pieces.

**3.** Pin and sew 2 collar pieces together along the outside edge, leaving the neck edge un-sewn. Repeat for the remaining collar pieces.

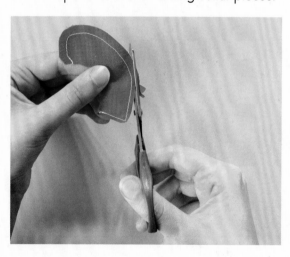

**4.** Trim the seam allowances to ⅛″ (3mm) and trim diagonally at the corners. Turn the collars right side out and press.

**5.** Pin and baste the collars to the right side of the bodice, with the collars meeting at the center front.

**6.** Pin and sew the bodice to the bodice lining at the neckline, with the collars sandwiched between them (see Sewing Curves, page 21). Cut triangle-shaped notches within the seam allowances.

**7.** Turn the bodice right side out and press. Baste all the *raw* edges just inside the ¼″ (6mm) seam allowance, sewing through both the bodice and the lining.

## Sleeves

**1.** Sew gathering stitches on the curved edge of the sleeves and gather to fit the bodice (see Gathering, page 20).

**2.** Pin and sew the sleeves to the bodice, concentrating the gathers at the top of the curve (see Sewing Sleeves, page 21). Finish the seam allowances.

**3.** Sew gathering stitches on the lower edge of the sleeves and gather to fit the sleeve bands (see Gathering, page 20).

**4.** Fold and press the sleeve bands in half lengthwise, wrong sides together.

**5.** Pin and sew the bands to the sleeve ends. Finish the seam allowances and press them toward the sleeve. Photo shows the sleeve finish detail only; the sleeve should be sewn to the bodice first.

## Finish

**1.** Follow Vintage Party Dress, View A; Finish; Steps 1–5.

**2.** Hand baste the collar toward the bodice, sewing through the lining, bodice, and only the underside of the collar, so the stitches do not show on the outside.

## *Vintage Party Dress, View C*

### Bodice

**1.** Fold the bodice front in half with wrong sides together and press.

**2.** Sew ⅜″ (1cm) from the center fold. Open and press the fold flat. Edgestitch on both sides to create the mock placket (see Swing Tank Tops, Mock Placket in Top Front, Steps 1–3, page 43).

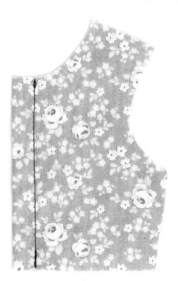

**3.** Follow Vintage Party Dress, View B; Bodice and Collar; Steps 1–7 (page 80).

### Sleeves

**1.** Sew gathering stitches on the curved edge of the sleeves and gather to fit the bodice (see Gathering, page 20).

**2.** Pin and sew the sleeves to the bodice, concentrating the gathers at the top of the curve (for tips, see Sewing Sleeves, page 21). Finish the seam allowances.

**3.** Sew gathering stitches on the lower edge of the sleeves and gather to fit the sleeve binding pieces (see Gathering, page 20).

**4.** Fold and press one long edge of the binding piece ¼″ (6mm) to the wrong side.

**5.** Pin and sew the unfolded edge of the binding to the lower edge of the sleeve, with the right side of the binding piece facing the wrong side of the sleeve ends. Photo shows the sleeve finish detail only; the sleeve should be sewn to the bodice first.

**6.** Fold the binding piece to the right side of the sleeve, enclosing all the raw edges. Press and sew the binding to the sleeve.

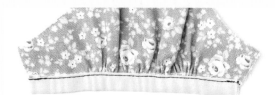

### Finish

**1.** Follow Vintage Party Dress, View A; Finish; Step 1 to sew the bodice side seams.

**2.** Fold the skirt piece in half at the center with wrong sides together and press. Sew ⅜″ (1cm) from the center fold.

**3.** Open the skirt pieces and press the fold flat. Edgestitch on both sides to create the mock placket.

**4.** Follow Vintage Party Dress, View A; Finish; Steps 2–7, aligning the mock plackets at the front.

**5.** Hand baste the collar to the bodice, sewing through the lining, bodice, and only the underside of the collar, so the stitches do not show on the outside.

**6.** Sew the buttons on the front plackets.

**7.** Tie the ribbon sash around the waist.

# Fitted T-Shirt and Fit and Flare Dress

A

B

A: SKILL LEVEL ◉ ◉ ◉
B: SKILL LEVEL ◉ ◉ ◉

**TIP** *Sewing with Knit Fabrics*

Don't be hesitant to sew knit garments. They are not diffi-cult, just different. In my beginning sewing classes for kids, I try to make sure each child sews at least one knit project.

A FEW TIPS:

- Choose a medium-weight stretch knit fabric. Avoid cotton interlock knits.

- Sew soon after cutting out the fabric pieces. The longer the fabric sits, the more the edges curl.

- Sew with a stretch needle and stretch stitch setting.

- Reduce the presser foot pressure.

- Use ballpoint pins.

**MATERIALS**

*Suggested fabrics: cotton Lycra or spandex*

DRESS AND T-SHIRT: ¼ yard (22.9cm) of stretch knit fabric

HOOK-AND-LOOP TAPE (⅜″/1CM WIDE): ¼ yard (22.9cm)

SEWING KIT (page 7)

## CUTTING

*Use the patterns to cut out the fabric and lining pieces (see Using a Pattern, page 11). Follow the cutting instructions on the patterns and use a fabric-marking tool to transfer any pattern markings onto the fabric pieces.*

View A

- Fitted T-Shirt Front 18

- Fitted T-Shirt Back 19

View B

- Fitted T-Shirt Front 18

- Fitted T-Shirt Back 19

- Fit and Flare Dress Skirt 20

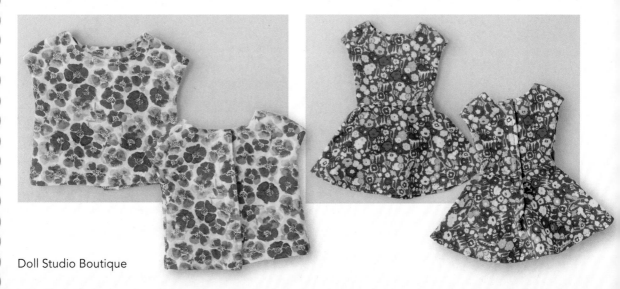

# SEWING INSTRUCTIONS

*All seam allowances are ¼″ (6mm) unless otherwise instructed. Sew seams and hems with a stretch stitch, such as a narrow zigzag stitch.*

## Fitted T-Shirt, View A

**1.** Pin the front and back pieces together at the shoulders, with right sides together and the raw edges even.

**2.** Sew together the shoulder seams. Press the seam allowances open.

**3.** Press the neckline edge ¼″ (6mm) to the wrong side and sew across the folded fabric.

**4.** Press the sleeve ends ¼″ (6mm) to the wrong side and sew across the folded fabric.

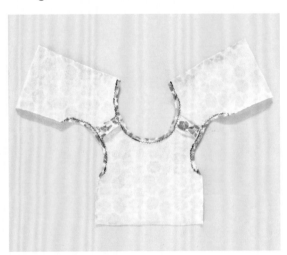

**5.** Fold the T-shirt right sides together and align the side edges. Pin and sew the side seams.

**6.** Fold the lower edge ⅜″ (1cm) to the wrong side and press.

**7.** Sew across the folded fabric.

Fitted T-Shirt and Fit and Flare Dress

**8.** Sew the center back closure (see Fully Open Back, page 22).

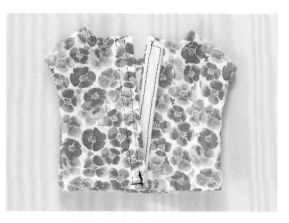

---

*Fit and Flare Dress, View B*

**1.** Follow Fitted T-Shirt, View A, Steps 1–5.

**2.** Pin and sew the skirt piece to the lower edge of the bodice. Press the seam allowances toward the bodice.

**3.** Sew the center back seam and closure (see Partially Open Back, page 23).

**4.** Hem the dress by folding the lower edge ⅜″ (1cm) to the wrong side and press.

**5.** Sew across the folded fabric.

# PJ Sets and ♥ Nightgown

You can mix and match a variety of different tops to go with the PJ bottoms. The Swing Tank Top, shown on page 88, or the Fitted T-Shirt (page 83) or even the Raglan Top (page 45) all make for a cute PJ set. The bottoms are also a nice project for Confident Beginners to learn how to sew piping details.

A: SKILL LEVEL ◖◗ ◖
B: SKILL LEVEL ◗ ◗ ◗
C: SKILL LEVEL ◗ ◗ ◗

Consider adding a graphic to your top using TAP (Transfer Artist Paper from C&T Publishing)! I made this graphic using the icons in Microsoft Word and my printer. TAP is easy to use; it came out perfect the first try! I love the results and I think it helps the PJ set look coordinated. You can see other examples of how I used TAP for the tops in Simple Shorts and Pants (page 50) and Headbands (page 98).

## MATERIALS

*Suggested fabric: quilting cotton*

### All views

PIPING OR ZIPPER PRESSER FOOT for Views B and C

SEWING KIT (page 7)

### Views A and C

PJ TOP FABRIC: Fat quarter
(approximately 18″ × 22″/45.7 × 55.9cm)

PJ TOP LINING: Lightweight scrap 5″ × 10″
(12.7 × 25.4cm)

PJ SHORTS OR PANTS: Fat quarter
(approximately 18″ × 22″/45.7 × 55.9cm)

LACE (¼″–½″/6–12MM WIDE) OR PIPING:
16″ (40.6cm) for both top and pants

ELASTIC (⅛″/3MM WIDE): ¼ yard (22.9cm)

### View B

NIGHTGOWN:
¼ yard (22.9cm)

LINING: 5″ × 10″
(12.7 × 25.4cm)

PIPING
(¼″–½″/6–12MM WIDE):
4″ (10.2cm)

ELASTIC
(⅛″/3MM WIDE):
¼ yard (22.9cm)

## CUTTING

*Use the patterns to cut out the fabric and
lining pieces (see Using a Pattern, page 11).
Follow the cutting instructions on the patterns
and use a fabric-marking tool to transfer
any pattern markings onto the fabric pieces.
Use the measurements provided to cut out
the remaining pieces (see Cut Fabric Pieces
Without Patterns, page 13).*

### All views

- PJ Top/Nightgown Yoke Front 36
- PJ Top/Nightgown Yoke Back 37
- PJ Top/Nightgown Sleeve 38

## View A

- PJ Bottoms 39
- PJ Top/Nightgown: 3″ × 17″ (7.6 × 43.2cm)

## View B

- Nightgown: 6½″ × 20″ (16.5 × 50.8cm)

## View C

- PJ Top/Nightgown: 3″ × 17″ (7.6 × 43.2cm)
- PJ Bottoms 39
- Cuff: 2″ × 5¼″ (5.1 × 13.3cm); cut 2.

**TIP** *Make a Custom-Length Nightgown*
To determine the best length for the nightgown, sew the yoke and put it onto your doll, and then measure from the lower edge to the length you would like. Add ¼″ (6mm) for the seam allowance and ⅓–½″ (8–12mm) for hemming.

# SEWING INSTRUCTIONS

*All seam allowances are ¼˝ (6mm) and fabric is placed with right sides together, unless otherwise instructed.*

## PJ Top and Nightgown, Views A, B, and C

### Shoulders/Back Yoke

**1.** Pin and sew the yoke back pieces to the yoke lining back pieces at the neck and upper back edges (see Sewing Curves, page 21).

**2.** Trim the seam allowance at the pivot point.

**3.** Turn right side out and press.

**TIP** For nice round edges and crisp corners, press the seam allowances toward the outside fabric with the tip of the iron in between the 2 layers of fabric *before turning the pieces right side out.*

---

### Front Yoke

**1.** Pin and sew the lace trim (View A) or piping (Views B and C) to the upper edge of the yoke front with right sides together. Use a piping or zipper presser foot when sewing the piping.

**TIP** For additional help, watch my video tutorial about sewing piping; for the link, see Bonus Videos (page 112).

**TIP** If the lace trim has extra seam allowance, trim it off before sewing to the project. Cut it ¼″ (6mm) from the edge of the design so the raw edges of the fabric and lace will be even.

**2.** Pin and baste the yoke back to the yoke front with right sides together.

**3.** Pin and sew the front yoke lining to the yoke front, with the right side of the lining facing the right side of the yoke front and the yoke backs sandwiched between.

**4.** Turn the yoke front right side out and press, with the lace/trim pressed up away from the yoke and lining. Baste the raw edges.

## Sleeves

**1.** Make a casing on the sleeve ends, with the first fold ¼″ (6mm) and the second fold ⅜″ (1cm). Stitch close to the second fold (see Sew a Casing for Elastic, page 18).

**2.** Sew gathering stitches along the curved edge and gather to fit the arm opening in the yoke (see Gathering, page 20).

**3.** Pin and sew the sleeves to the yoke (see Sewing Sleeves, page 21). Finish the seam allowances and press them toward the sleeve

**4.** Insert the elastic (2⅞″/7.3cm for each sleeve) into the casings. Secure the elastic by sewing across the casing and the elastic.

## Side Seams

**1.** Fold the yoke unit in half, right sides together, and sew the side and sleeve seam in one continuous seam, pivoting at the underarm/sleeve seam.

**2.** Finish the seam allowances and press them toward the back.

## Skirt

**1.** Hem the lower edge of the skirt piece with a ½″ (12mm) hem allowance (see Double-Fold Hem, page 16).

**2.** Sew gathering stitches on the upper edge and gather to fit the Yoke (see Gathering, page 20).

**3.** Pin and sew the skirt piece to the yoke. Finish the seam allowances and press them up toward the yoke. Topstitch.

## Back Closure

**1.** Finish the raw edges of the center back.

**2.** Sew the center back closure to the PJ top (see Fully Open Back, page 22).

**3.** Sew the center back seam and closure to the nightgown (see Partially Open Back, page 23).

## PJ Shorts, View A, and PJ Pants, View C

### View A

**1.** Pin and sew the lace to the lower edge of the shorts with the raw edges even.

**2.** Finish the seam allowances and press them toward the waist. *Optional:* Topstitch.

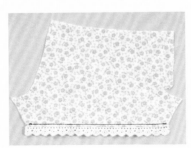

**3.** Refer to Shorts, View A, and Pants, View B; Steps 3–11 (pages 52–54), to finish the shorts.

**TIP** It is easier to make the PJ pants and shorts without the mock fly detail.

## View C

**1.** Fold the cuff piece in half lengthwise with wrong sides together. Press.

**2.** Pin and sew the piping to the top edge of the cuff piece with all raw edges even. Use a piping or zipper foot when sewing the piping.

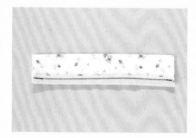

**3.** Pin and sew the cuff piece to the lower edge of the pants, keeping all the raw edges even.

**4.** Finish the seam allowances and press them up toward the pants. *Optional:* Topstitch.

**5.** Refer to Shorts, View A, and Pants, View B; Steps 3–11 (pages 52–54) to finish the pants.

**TIP** For a slightly easier project, simply hem the PJ pants and shorts instead of using trim or cuffs (see Double-Fold Hem, page 16). Use the longest-length cutting line for the pieces.

# Slippers

Accessories make playtime so much fun! These cozy slippers are the perfect accessory to complete your doll's bedtime outfit.

SKILL LEVEL ⊙ ⊙ ⊙ ⊙

### MATERIALS

SLIPPERS: Fabric scraps

FAST2FUSE/FUSIBLE BATTING: Small scrap

SEWING KIT (page 7)

### CUTTING

*Use the patterns to cut out the fabric pieces. Follow the cutting instructions on the patterns and use a fabric-marking tool to transfer any pattern markings onto the fabric pieces.*

• Slipper Top 40

• Slipper Base/Sole 41

• Slipper Binding 42

• Slipper Interfacing 43

**Note** The binding must be cut on the bias, otherwise it won't properly mold to the curved edges of the slippers (see Layout, Pin, and Cut the Patterns, page 12).

## SEWING INSTRUCTIONS

*All seam allowances are ¼˝ (6mm) and fabric is placed with right sides together, unless otherwise instructed.*

**1.** Pin and sew 2 top pieces together along the straight edge.

**2.** Turn right side out and press.

**3.** Repeat Steps 1 and 2 for the remaining 2 top pieces.

**4.** Fuse fast2fuse or batting to the wrong side of 2 base pieces that will be the sole of the slipper. As you make the slippers, make sure you have a left and a right slipper.

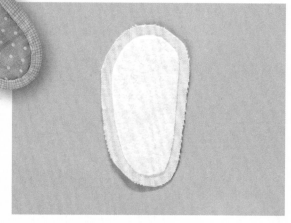

**5.** Baste together the base pieces ⅛″ (3mm) from the raw edge, with wrong sides together and the interfacing in the middle.

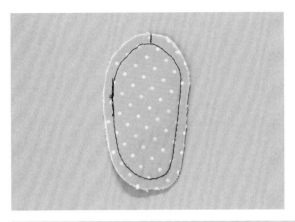

**6.** Pin the top to the base, taking care to align the pattern markings and keep the raw edges even. Sew the top to the base, using an ⅛″ (3mm) seam allowance or less.

**7.** Fold and press one long and one short edge of the binding strip ¼″ (6mm) to the wrong side.

**8.** Pin the long unfolded edge of the binding strip to the top of the slipper base. Start with the short folded end on the inside side edge of the slipper.

**9.** Sew the binding to the slipper using ⅛″ (3mm) seam allowance, sewing slowly and keep the raw edges even.

**10.** Fold and wrap the bias strip to the sole of the slipper, enclosing the raw edges. Hand sew the binding to the soles, being careful to not stitch through the base or top.

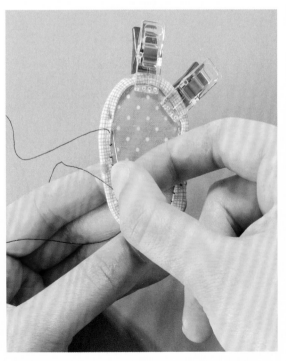

# Headbands

A

B

C

A: SKILL LEVEL
B: SKILL LEVEL
C: SKILL LEVEL

## MATERIALS

*Suggested fabrics (Views B and C): quilting cotton or lightweight woven fabric*

**All views**

SEWING KIT (page 7)

**View A**

RIBBON (⅜″/1CM WIDE): ½ yard (45.7cm)

ELASTIC (¼″/6MM WIDE): 1½″ (3.8cm)

ANTI-FRAY SEALANT

FABRIC GLUE OR WONDER TAPE

**Views B and C**

HEADBAND: Scraps of fabric

**View B**

ELASTIC (¼″/6MM WIDE): 1½″

**View C**

ELASTIC (¼″/6MM WIDE): 3″

## CUTTING

Use the patterns to cut out the fabric pieces (see Using a Pattern, page 11). Follow the cutting instructions on the patterns and use a fabric-marking tool to transfer any pattern markings onto the fabric pieces. Use the measurements provided to cut out other pieces (see Cut Fabric Pieces Without Patterns, page 13).

**View A**

**View B**

• Headband: 1⅝″ × 8½″ (4.1 × 21.6cm)

**View C**

• Headband 44

Photos by Sydney Paulsen

# SEWING INSTRUCTIONS

*All seam allowances are ¼˝ (6mm) and fabric is placed with right sides together, unless otherwise instructed.*

## View A

*This headband can be made with or without the bow.*

**1.** Cut the ribbon into 3 pieces: 8½˝ (21.6cm), 5¼˝ (13.3cm), and 4¼˝ (10.8cm). Seal the ends of the 2 larger pieces with anti-fray sealant.

**2.** Fold the ends of the 5¼˝ (13.3cm) length of ribbon to the center on one side, overlapping the ends at least ¼˝ (6mm).

**3.** Sew together at the center, sewing through all 3 layers.

**4.** Wrap the 4¼˝ (10.8cm) length of ribbon around the center of the bow. Use fabric glue or Wonder Tape to hold in place. Sew across the sides of the wrapped ribbon and cut away the excess ribbon. Seal the end with anti-fray sealant

**5.** Sew the bow to the remaining ribbon piece, 3½˝ (8.9cm) from one end.

**6.** Sew the ends of the elastic piece to the ribbon ends.

## View B

**1.** Fold and press the short ends of the headband pieces ¼″ (6mm) to the wrong side of the fabric. Sew across the folded fabric.

**2.** Fold in half lengthwise and sew together. Trim the seam allowances to ⅛″ (3mm).

**3.** Pin a safety pin in the fabric at one of the openings and feed it inside the opening to turn the headband right side out easily. Press.

**4.** Place the ends of the elastic piece into the openings. Secure the elastic by sewing across the fabric and the elastic.

---

## View C

**1.** Fold and press the short ends of the headband pieces ¼″ (6mm) to the wrong side of the fabric.

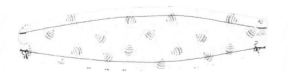

**2.** Pin and sew the headband pieces together. Trim the seam allowances to ⅛″ (3mm).

**3.** Turn the headband right side out and press.

**4.** Place the ends of the elastic piece into the openings. Secure the elastic by sewing across the fabric and the elastic.

# Tote Bags

**A:** SKILL LEVEL
**B:** SKILL LEVEL
**C:** SKILL LEVEL

## MATERIALS

*Suggested fabrics: quilting cotton and medium-weight woven fabric*

**All views**

SEWING KIT (page 7)

**Views A and C**

BAG: Fat quarter (approximately 18″ × 22″/45.7 × 55.9cm)

LINING: Fat quarter (approximately 18″ × 22″/45.7 × 55.9cm)

**View B**

BAG: Long scraps of 4 coordinating fabrics, at least 1″ × 10″ (2.5 × 25.4cm)

**View C**

RIBBON (⅛″/3MM WIDE): 10″ (25.4cm), cut into 2 pieces

## CUTTING

*Use the patterns to cut out the fabric and lining pieces (see Using a Pattern, page 11). Follow the cutting instructions on the patterns and use a fabric-marking tool to transfer any pattern markings onto the fabric pieces. Use the measurements provided to cut the remaining pieces (see Cut Fabric Pieces Without Patterns, page 13).*

**View A**

- Tote Bag 45
- Strap: 2″ × 7½″ (5.1 × 19.1cm); cut 2.

## View B

- Tote Bag 45 (Cut the pattern from pieced fabric and from lining fabric as indicated on pattern.)

- Strips: 1″ × 10″ (2.5 × 25.4cm); cut 1 each from 3 of the fabrics.

- Strip: 1¾″ × 10″ (4.4 × 25.4cm); cut 1 from 1 of the fabrics.

- Strap: 2″ × 12½″ (5.1 × 31.8cm); cut 2.

## View C

- Knot Handle Tote 46

## SEWING INSTRUCTIONS

*All seam allowances are ¼″ (6mm) and fabric is placed with right sides together, unless otherwise instructed.*

### View A

**1.** Pin and sew the bag pieces together at the side and bottom edges; back-stitch at the beginning and end of the seams. Do not sew the square cutouts at the lower corners. Press the seam allowances open.

**2.** Repeat Step 1 for the lining pieces, leaving an opening 1″–1½″ (2.5–3.8cm) along the bottom edge.

**3.** Fold the bag at the corners, matching the side and bottom seams and the raw edges. Sew the corners to make boxed corners.

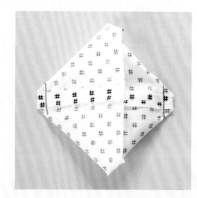

**4.** Repeat Step 3 for the lining.

**5.** Turn the lining *wrong* side out and the bag *right* side out. Place the bag inside the lining, with right sides together and the raw edges and side seams aligned. Sew together at the top edge.

*Note:* It most likely won't fit easily over the free arm of the sewing machine. Place it under the needle as shown below.

**6.** Reach inside the opening in the lining and pull the bag out until both the lining and bag are both turned right side out.

**7.** Sew the opening in the lining closed. If you sew the lining neatly by hand, the bag will be reversible.

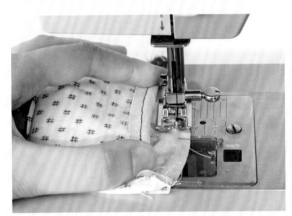

---

**8.** Tuck the lining inside the bag and press the entire bag.

**9.** Make the straps, each with 2 finished ends (see Make Straps, page 19).

**10.** Sew the straps to the inside of the bag, placing the outer edge of the straps 1″ (2.5cm) from the side seams.

## View B

**1.** Sew the long strips together with the wider strip at the bottom. Press the seam allowances open.

**2.** Cut the pieced strip set into 2 pieces, each 5″ (12.7cm) wide.

**3.** Cut 2 pieces using the Tote Bag 45 pattern. Keep the seams aligned at the raw edges when you fold the patchwork fabric to cut out the bag pieces.

**4.** Follow View A, Steps 1–9 to finish the bag and make the straps.

**5.** Tie the ends of the straps into knots and sew the straps to the outside of the bag.

### View C

**1.** Sew the ribbons to the right side at the center top edge of both bag pieces.

**2.** Follow View A, Steps 1–4, keeping in mind these side seams include the straps.

**3.** Turn the lining *wrong* side out and the bag *right* side out. Place the bag inside the lining, with right sides together and the raw edges aligned. Flatten the straps and align the seams.

**4.** Sew the bag to the lining on the curved top edges, including the straps. Round the corners at the ends of the straps.

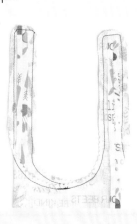

**5.** Follow View A, Steps 6–8 to finish the bag. Tie the straps together with a knot.

**TIP** Use a hemostat or long tweezers to help you pull the straps right side out. Or if you have a wooden knitting needle or chopstick, use the blunt end to push the straps right side out.

# Bucket Hat

These hats are so fun and make great accessories to any outfit. Careful pinning and sewing slowly are the most challenging bits to making this style of hat.

A: SKILL LEVEL
B: SKILL LEVEL
C: SKILL LEVEL

## MATERIALS

*Suggested fabrics: quilting cotton, seersucker, chambray, lightweight twill, or linen*

### All views

HAT: Fat quarter (approximately 18″ × 22″/45.7 × 55.9cm)

LINING: Large scraps of fabric (View B features contrast lining fabric.)

SEWING KIT (page 7)

### View A

RIBBON (⅜″/1CM WIDE): ¼ yard (22.9cm)

### View C

RIBBON (½″–⅝″/1.2–1.6CM WIDE): ⅛ yard (11.4cm)

## CUTTING

*Use the patterns to cut out the fabric pieces (see Using a Pattern, page 11). Follow the cutting instructions on the patterns and use a fabric-marking tool to transfer any pattern markings onto the fabric pieces.*

### All views

• Hat Crown 47

• Hat Side 48

### Views A

• Hat Brim 49

### View B

• Hat Brim 49

### View C

• Hat Brim 50

# SEWING INSTRUCTIONS

*All seam allowances are ¼˝ (6mm) and fabric is placed with right sides together, unless otherwise instructed.*

*Bucket Hat, Views A and B*

## Crown and Side Assembly

**1.** Sew a row of straight stitches on the upper edge of the side piece, just inside the ¼˝ (6mm) seam allowance.

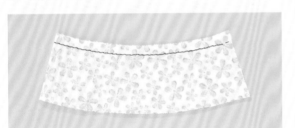

**2.** Sew the 2 short ends of the side piece together to form a loop. Press the seam allowances open.

**3.** Use small, sharp scissors to make vertical cuts every ⅜˝ (1cm) along the stitched edge, being careful not to cut the stitches.

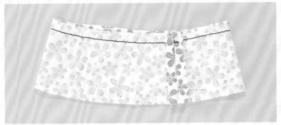

**4.** Pin the side piece to the crown piece in between the cuts in the seam allowance, keeping the raw edges even. The side-piece seam allowance will spread at the cuts. This is necessary for the 2 pieces to fit together evenly.

**5.** Carefully sew the side piece to the crown, being careful not to sew any tucks. Use a short stitch length and pivot slightly every 2–3 stitches as you remove each pin.

**6.** Finish the seam allowances and press toward the side piece. Topstitch.

## Brim

**1.** Sew the short ends of the brim piece together; press the seam allowances open.

**2.** Repeat Step 1 for the brim lining piece.

**3.** Pin and sew the brim lining to the brim piece on the outside edge, matching the seams.

**4.** Trim the seam allowances to ⅛″ (3mm). Turn right side out and press.

**5.** Baste the brim and brim lining together along the inner edge, just inside the ¼″ (6mm) seam allowance

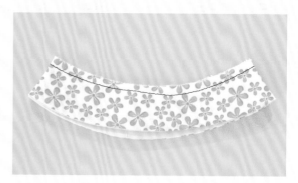

**6.** Follow Crown and Side Assembly, Steps 3–6 to sew the brim to the side of the hat. This time, cut every ¾″ (1.9cm) within the seam allowance of the brim piece before pinning it to the side piece.

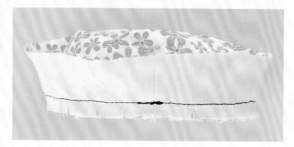

## Finish

For View A, sew the ribbon around the hat along the brim/side seam.

## View C

**1.** Follow Crown and Side Assembly, Steps 1–6.

**2.** Pin and sew the brim to the brim lining along the outer edges.

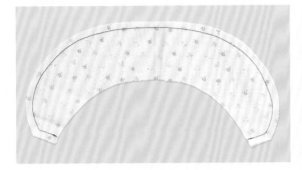

**3.** Trim the seam allowances to ⅛″ (3mm) and turn right side out. Press. Pressing the seam allowances toward the lining first helps to achieve an even curve all the way around.

**4.** Follow Crown and Side Assembly, Steps 3–6 to sew the brim to the side of the hat, with the short ends meeting at the side seam at the center back of the hat.

**5.** Tie the ribbon into a bow and sew it to the back of the hat.

# About the Author

Growing up, Erin Hentzel was surrounded by DIYers and sewists. She first held a needle and thread in her own hand at age seven. One ordinary Saturday afternoon, her dad brought home a vintage Singer. That afternoon he taught her to use a sewing machine, and she sewed her first project on it. This introduction at age ten kindled her need to create, fostering her lifelong love of sewing.

Erin is the creator and designer behind Avery Lane Designs, an indie sewing pattern company. She loves teaching others to sew and lives in a quiet college town within beautiful Willamette Valley, Oregon, with her husband; sweet Malamute, Lucy; and two kittens, Stanley and Oliver.

---

*Visit Erin online and follow on social media!*

**WEBSITE**
averylanesewing.com

**FACEBOOK**
/averylanedesigns

**ETSY SHOP**
etsy.com/shop/averylane

**INSTAGRAM**
@averylanesewing

**AVERY LANE PATTERNS SEWING GROUP**
facebook.com > *search* Avery Lane Patterns
Sewing Group
*Join Erin on Facebook to show off your creations, ask sewing questions, join sew-alongs, and enter design challenges!*

## Bonus Videos

Go to C&T Publishing's YouTube channel for video tutorials about turning a lined bodice right side out, sewing piping, and sewing a rolled hem!

youtube.com/user/candtpublishing >

▶ *search* Sleeveless Peplum Hem Top Tutorial for 18″ Dolls

▶ *search* How to Sew Piping

▶ *search* How to Sew Petite Hems for Doll Dresses

## ALSO BY ERIN HENTZEL